Reel Lessons In Leadership

RALPH R. DISIBIO

Foreword by Stephen Hanks
President & CEO
Washington Group International

Cover & book design by
Stephen Muller

THE PALADIN GROUP LLC
Aiken, South Carolina USA

Published by The Paladin Group LLC
123 Summer Squall Lane
Aiken, South Carolina 29803
email: publishpaladin@aol.com

Copyright 2006 by The Paladin Group LLC

Cover design and layout by Stephen Muller

Information courtesy of The Internet Movie Database
The following excerpts are reprinted with permission

Apollo 13
(http:www.imdb.com/title/tt0112384/quotes)
The Contender
(http:www.imdb.com/title/tt0068646/quotes)
Erin Brockovich
(http:www.imdb.com/title/tt0195685/quotes)
Gandhi
(http:www.imdb.com/title/tt0083987/quotes)
Glory
(http:www.imdb.com/title/tt0097441/quotes)
The Godfather
(http:www.imdb.com/title/tt0068646/quotes)
High Noon
(http:www.imdb.com/title/tt0044706/quotes)
Lawrence of Arabia
(http:www.imdb.com/title/tt0056172/quotes)
One Flew Over the Cuckoo's Nest
(http:www.imdb.com/title/tt0073486/quotes)
Patton
(http:www.imdb.com/title/tt0066206/quotes)
Seabiscuit
(http:www.imdb.com/title/tt0068646/quotes)

All right reserved. This book, or parts thereof,
may not be reproduced in any form without permission.

Printed in the United States of America

ISBN 0-9779273-0-X

Library of Congress Control Number: 2006902370

This book is dedicated to my family

They are the wind in my sails in calm seas
and my anchor in troubled waters

CREDITS
People Who've Made a Difference

I am indebted to many who have made this endeavor a reality. First and foremost, without the tireless efforts of Stephen Muller, this book would not have its look or feel. More importantly, his encouragement, creativity and style kept me focused and challenged. He is the one person who was involved from concept to fruition, and his contribution was enormous.

Don Allen, my fraternity brother from decades past and an author of some note, inspired me to take up this cause. He reviewed and commented on several sections.

I thank James Lieber, a friend and accomplished author, who saw "adaptability" in *Lawrence of Arabia*.

Patti Piech, English teacher extraordinaire, took up the thankless task of editing some early chapters in her usual modest but expert way.

I am forever indebted to all of those executives with whom I have had the privilege to work over the years. My days in education, government and at three great corporations—Westinghouse, Parsons and Washington Group International—exposed me to some great leaders, each of whom had an impact on my performance and philosophy. Joe Mazzarella, Dr. Thomas Sykes, Barry Koh, Ted Stern, Tom Anderson, the late Chris Schaller, the late Len Pieroni and the late Joe Volpe are right up there on my leadership talent and mentor list.

The leadership talent to which I have been exposed at Washington Group International has been most instrumental in the development of this project as well as my personal development. Tom Zarges, Steve Johnson, George Juetten, Lou Pardi and E. Preston Rahe were major contributors to that development, as were Charles Oliver and Vince Kontny. Dennis Washington's wisdom and instinct brought me to the visionary leadership of Stephen Hanks and his remarkable achievements in turning a crippled corporation into a successful, growing company. I wish all aspiring leaders could have the benefit of being exposed to these exceptional leaders.

Special mention and thanks are also deserved by those who directly assisted me when I took on important leadership roles. These are some of the people who justly deserve much of the spotlight that I garnered. While they toiled diligently, often in anonymity, to keep up with my frenetic pace, I was the beneficiary of their labor and support. Chris Verenes, Jennifer Large, Steve Marchetti, Natale Girgenti, Frank Caterini and the late Eileen Sheedy are most vivid in this regard. Of course, to those who have opined on this book after early review, and are quoted herein, I express my appreciation as well.

Last, but certainly not least, one's spouse, of course, plays a defining role in projects of this magnitude. I have been lucky to have a mate who not only tolerated the sacrifice of the time I devoted to developing, executing, talking about and rethinking, ad nauseam, every facet of this book but, because of superior intellect, also contributed mightily to the syntax, the spelling and the structure of the book. Carol is "The Queen of Rewrites."

CONTENTS
What You'll Find Inside

FOREWORD
The Noblest Art of All

Like many of you, I've long been a student of great leaders—men and women of influence and impact who come in exceedingly different packages, with unique backgrounds, skill sets, and approaches and varying degrees of effectiveness. Many of them are models of excellence and of noble character.

One of those leaders is Harry Morrison, the man that *TIME Magazine* featured on the cover of its May 3, 1954, edition. At the time, Harry was the president of one of Washington Group International's heritage companies, Morrison-Knudsen. Harry was a man of incredible vision, determination and honor. In the 1920's, his company used bulldozers and diesel trucks instead of horses to revolutionize the building of dams in the Pacific Northwest. Later, he formed a coalition of companies to embark on a construction project called by some the eighth wonder of the modern world: Hoover Dam.

TIME Magazine called Harry the one builder in history who had done the most to change the face of the earth. One of his favorite sayings was, "To build is the noblest art of all."

I've often wondered if Harry was referring to the structures he and his compatriots built or to the people he nurtured through his outstanding leadership.

It's a question I often pose to Washington Group International managers attending company classes on leadership and project management. "Are we here to build great projects," I ask, "or are we here to build the leadership of the future, to inspire the people we lead to greatness?"

The answer, in my experience, is all about what leaders are and what they do.

Washington Group International was recently named one of the top 20 corporations in the United States for developing leaders, along with 3M, GE and Johnson & Johnson. We were the only company in our industry. Among the reasons for that honor is our Leaders Forum where our current and aspiring leaders participate in an intensive week-long program of strategy, market trends, values and leadership. There we use a number of noted, outside speakers to engage participants in discussions about leadership. One of those speakers—and the author of this book—is Dr. Ralph DiSibio who has presented at the Forum since its inception. More than 400 executives have been exposed to his unique talents and ways of looking at leaders, their style and effectiveness—something you'll experience in the chapters that follow.

This book, *Reel Lessons in Leadership,* is about studying leadership greatness (and not-so-greatness) through the unique medium of film. Hollywood has created an unparalleled platform here. And Ralph is a master at carving meaning out of simply observing others—a unique leadership trait in itself.

Ralph is a long-time personal friend and colleague of mine. When he asked me to write the introduction to this book, I was honored because his unflinching leadership during some very difficult financial times for our company helped us keep our heads above water, focus on the goal, and come out a successful, growing company. And if that seems like another leadership trait, you're right! Take a look at the chapter on *Apollo 13.*

Yet, as you read this book and think about the characters described in it, remember that leadership is a very personal thing. Henry Fonda's down-home, patient style worked in the jury room in *12 Angry Men*. And George Patton's take-charge, no-holds-barred approach to war turned a rag-tag group of soldiers into a fighting machine. But the two leadership styles probably would not be interchangeable in the same situations.

But you don't need to be Fonda or Patton. You need to be yourself. Build on your strengths. Tap the strengths of others. Lead by example. In fact, I'd say that's the single leadership trait that is common to all great leaders: they set an example for others. That kind of willingness to do what we say—with words and actions consistent—is the glue that builds teams and winning organizations.

Leadership comes in many forms. It is not tied to position or level in an organization, and it is something that can be improved.

Leaders inspire others, they build others up, and they praise the behaviors they seek and admire in others. They are also tough when they need to be.

Leaders observe, they emulate others. They listen, they learn. But most of all, they seek to make a difference. In Harry Morrison's words, they're about "betterment." I like to believe that at Washington Group International we don't build things, we develop people who build things. This book is a tool in developing our people. May it also serve you well as you make a difference in your world.

Stephen G. Hanks, President and CEO
Washington Group International

I'VE GOT A SECRET

Take command!

Everyone has the answer. Jack Welch, Lee Iacocca, Bill Gates, Steven Covey, Larry Bossidy and hundreds of others, men and women who have made it to the top of the corporate ladder think that they've found the secret to leadership success. The enigma of leadership, and discovery of the magic key to unlock the door to the leadership puzzle, requires only reading the latest books by them. Most everyone certainly respects these successful captains of industry and the hundreds of aspiring captains, but, with all due respect, there are no secrets.

Just take a look at the *New York Times* list of best selling non-fiction. On any given list, it's not unusual to find that half of the top thirty books deal with leadership or self-improvement leading to promotion or management or career advancement. Amble through the Barnes & Noble business section, and scan the hundreds of books alluding to the subject. Every airport news shop prominently displays the latest revelation on how to achieve corporate success through a variety of leadership styles: quiet leadership, leadership by the Huns, hidden leadership, leadership through service, gut reaction leadership, the habits of successful leaders. And on and on it goes, seemingly non-stop.

These tomes all contain pearls of wisdom to be sure. In fact, you might well conclude that the cumulative knowledge in all of these publications, if absorbed, adopted and dutifully practiced, would make you a crown prince, if not a king or queen. Of course, none of the authors suggests that you can adopt, or even adapt, all of the lessons offered. Yet, there is one truth that is universal in all of these treatments: *leadership counts.*

The ills and the health of any organization can be laid directly at the door of the executive suite, and I do not believe there is any exception to this fact. Check for yourself. Each year, well-known financial journals list the top 20 or 100 of the "best places to work." There are numerous factors on which companies are judged, ranging from employee benefits to workplace ambiance. But when it comes right down to it, the leadership of those companies is directly responsible for each one of the factors.

It is no coincidence that every merger and acquisition director identifies effective management/leadership as a prime requirement for targeting a particular company. When it comes to putting their money where their mouths are, decision-makers know that it's leadership that counts.

With all that's been written about the subject, the myriad of popular books and articles that inundate us today with the how-to's and wherefore's of running companies offer negligible practical examples that we can use to understand the qualities or traits that need to be developed if one is to be a leader. Rather, they offer a variety of hints, exercises, personalized vignettes and snippets of effective leadership and management actions and styles. They all suffer from the same elementary shortcoming in that they are basically theoretical. They tell us what we should do or what particular leaders did to succeed. The lessons are often enlightening and sometimes entertaining in a story-like way. At the end of the day...or the chapter or the book...it is left to the reader to imagine the defining events or episodes and to put them in the context that the writer experienced or intended.

When Jack shares with us his philosophy in action when he tells the story of firing an individual in the lowest ten percent of the upper echelon, we are left to imagine the expressions, the body language or the mood. This book is designed to add what has been missing in the collection of leadership treatments that have gone before. The goal is to provide the missing context without ambiguity and offer the reader an avenue to observe, like the proverbial fly on the wall, leadership traits and qualities in the "reel" world.

An Early Career Lesson

As an aspiring manager and a leader myself for more than forty years, I have observed what leaders do to lead and how managers manage. On my journey from teaching to becoming a corporate executive with many stops in between, I've tried to identify and practice leadership skills with diligence, in part by careful observation as others applied those same skills. Finally, after a couple of decades in which I had the good fortune to serve as the president of major corporate business units, I have returned, in retirement, to teach upper level managers and leaders about the qualities of leadership. I am not so much attempting to teach people to lead but, rather, to provide some insight about what qualities leaders have in common and how those qualities are drawn upon in carrying on a business. In developing the course I teach, I felt that I needed an approach which was non-traditional. I personally knew many of the leaders I was asked to teach, indeed many had worked for me in the past. I wanted to offer them a view of leadership that would not only stimulate their thinking but would alter the way they observed—and performed—acts of leadership as well.

After much thought about how to go about this, I decided to use film clips to present dramatic examples of specific qualities of leadership. From the very first class, the high-performance leaders with whom I shared some of my ideas have reacted with enthusiasm and excitement as they've looked at films and at leadership as we will look at them in the chapters that follow. The dialogue, prompted by considering various leadership qualities shown by movie characters, has been vibrant and energetic, and each class has had a new take on the episodes and the impressions that they make.

I hope that you will have some of the same reactions as you use the films that are discussed to experience the qualities of leadership enacted with all the power of presentation that Hollywood can muster. I encourage you to watch the films that are discussed so that, like the people who have come to my classes, you can see Marlon Brando and George C. Scott and other characters literally acting out the leadership qualities that are being explored. When you think about it, I am convinced that you will see that the individual qualities that are depicted are the same qualities required in the corporate world, indeed in life, to succeed.

Observing these qualities in the full context of the film can provide a unique opportunity to be that fly on the wall as scenes unfold and you are able to witness the expressions and the body language that accompany a particular quality. You will actually *see* what is only left to the imagination in other approaches.

You may want to know a little about me before you invest your time in reading this book. Like all of us, I am the sum of my experiences with attributes and baggage that I bring to the table in every encounter. I have worked in many capacities: industrial labor union member, public school teacher and superintendent, chief contract negotiator, state cabinet officer, business developer, U.S. patent holder, business owner, project manager and corporate executive for Fortune 100 companies. There is no need to bore you with the details of these experiences, but suffice it to say that as someone charged with leadership in many environments, I have observed and learned from labor zealots, consummate bureaucrats, cutthroat salespeople, ambitious corporate managers, brilliant executives and billionaire entrepreneurs. Not every quality I saw in them was one that I would want to call my own. But there was something to be learned from everyone, and I was fortunate to have mentors who helped to shape my experiences as I learned to discern the traits that I would need to become better at whatever challenge I was offered. From the outset, I made it my business to really study and practice the qualities of leadership and the traits required for success, and I believe that that study and practice has served me well.

My first real leadership lesson came with my first permanent job. After attaining my undergraduate degree, I became a teacher, one of the few careers that is based on the assumption that the mere act of graduating puts you at the top of the profession. This was proven on day one when, fresh out of college with a lifetime teaching certification in New Jersey, I closed the door of my history classroom to face, alone, thirty high school students for the next fifty minutes. At that moment, I was the master of all I surveyed, or so I thought. What would I do with my first professional leadership challenge? As I said, it was to be my first lesson. I remembered one of my professors giving us a hint, "If the windows are open, close them; and if the lights are on, turn them off. Take command!" I did exactly that. When a young tough with his cigarettes rolled up in his sleeve asked to go to the "lav," I replied, "You can go, but leave your cigarettes on my desk." The student looked hurt and said, "I'm not gonna smoke." "Good," I said, "then you won't need them." And with that I was off on forty-plus years of practicing and observing leadership techniques, both good and bad.

Setting the Tone

The leadership of every organization sets the tone which creates the personality of that organization. All the other elements and aspects of the organization, including the unions, the make-up of the workforce, the geographic location of the business, the market forces and the economy, are merely the supporting cast for the star of the show, the leader. The tone the leader sets reflects, to be sure, the style of the individual and markedly influences the productive capability of the enterprise. The tone of an organization is something that we can observe and experience every day and in every dealing with a business.

Who can deny that there is a certain tone in a Starbucks or at a Nordstrom department store? A certain tone is also apt to be evident on the other end of the phone during a call to L.L. Bean or across the counter at the U.S. Postal Service. There is also a tone, perhaps shaped in part by the infrequent dealings with the public, at a Boeing factory. Make no mistake, at all of these locations the tone is largely set by leadership. We might not be able to define it, but we sense it and experience it and are left with some negative or positive impression as a result. J.D. Powers make its millions surveying how people respond to organizations, so we know it is something that can be measured.

This book explores in detail the qualities of leadership which ultimately make up the tone of a particular leader and the group that he or she leads. Using the examples provided by characters in movies, the book will show how certain of those qualities can impact results and performance.

Like many of my generation, I worked my way through college. I was fortunate to come from a home town of abundant industrial resources in a time when the United States was still a manufacturing juggernaut. Camden, New Jersey was then a hub of industry, the home of the Campbell Soup Company, the New York Shipbuilding Corporation, RCA Victor, the Esterbrook Pen Company and JR Evans Leather Company, among others. Recently, Camden was named the murder capital of America and the #1 crime city in the U.S., but that perhaps is the subject of some other book on lack of leadership.

I worked at both Campbell Soup and New York Shipbuilding, where—in short order—the leadership and the tones that they established became abundantly clear. It was difficult to define then and necessitates more words than seem required even today, but there was a striking contrast between these two businesses. The time which ended the first shift, 4:00 p.m., was the only thing these thriving corporations had in common. Everything else was different. The tone was different.

At a quarter to four in the afternoon, each of the thirty time clocks at the entrance/exit of the shipyard had long lines forming, with the first man in line balancing his timecard above the slot that would grab the card and enter the time it was inserted, keeping an electronic running tally of the time in and the time out each day to calculate the total hours worked and thus result in a paycheck. Not one minute before, for this would end up in reducing the paycheck by fifteen minutes, nor one minute after, for this would count for nothing except spending one more minute in hell, the worker would thrust the card in the machine for the imprinting of the time. Within fifteen minutes, five thousand men had exited the site with only the dust of their cars remaining as a testament to their attendance, so hurried was their escape.

Meanwhile, at the Campbell Soup plant, a whistle blew at 4:00 p.m. and the machinery of the cookers and the label machines and the like would slowly grind to a halt. The men and women would amble to the locker rooms, strip off their tan uniforms and don their street clothes amidst conversations of the shift's successes and tribulations. They would often stop by the cafeteria and commiserate over a last cup of coffee with the incoming shift, sharing cautions about the idiosyncrasies of certain machines or problems faced during the day.

The unmistakable difference in the two industrial giants was created by the different tones set by their leadership. That tone manifested itself in many ways. The "yard" was dirty, bereft of any hint of social amenities, driven by government contracts and controlled by powerful unions. The only communication was likely to be a grievance filed by the union or a new dictate pronounced by a paternalistic, invisible "management." The workforce spent much of the day dreaming up innovative ways not to work. Employees could get lost on purpose going from one end of the super-aircraft carrier Kitty Hawk or below deck on the NS Savannah, the world's first atomic cargo ship. They became really expert at this task—and

I, being a quick learner, got lost with the best of them. It was, sadly, almost a core value.

At Campbell's, by contrast, there was great pride in seeing your label at the local market and in maximizing production, in part because it showed up in your paycheck as a premium. Workers could share in the vision of the company which was communicated frequently in newsletters and bulletins. The foremen walked their spaces. Here, cleanliness was practiced personally and industrially as a core value. The differences were stark, and the impacts were real. The Campbell Soup Company, of course, still thrives today, but New York Shipbuilding foundered in the seventh decade of the 20th century.

I will seek in this book to share the lessons learned from a lifetime of observing and practicing the qualities which manifested themselves in the tones of those two corporations.

Observing Leaders In Action

Reference is constantly made to "leadership," but the very term defies practical definition. *The American Heritage Dictionary* defines it thusly: "1. The position or office of a leader. 2. The capacity to lead." A *leader* in the same text is defined as: "1. One that leads or guides. 2. One in charge or in command."

It is worthy of note that no corporation has a Chief Leader or VP of Leaders or Director of Leadership. Alas, a leadership definition, not unlike a definition of the "tone" discussed earlier, is somewhat elusive. I have studied many books, read hundreds of articles and attended conferences too numerous to mention on the subject. Particularly when reading about the experiences of a scion of industry, I have wished, as I keep saying, that I could have been a fly on the wall when events that are described were taking place. I could only imagine the context that might have been supplied by personal observation. That personal observation is what I hope to offer you here.

While a simple, all-encompassing definition of leadership is hard to come by, the qualities of leadership do lend themselves to identification and definition. There is near universal agreement on the various qualities that are exhibited by effective leaders. There are many qualities that leaders need to develop, to nurture and to hone in order to maximize their performance. There are many motion pictures with performances, by actors who may not be leaders but who demonstrate one quality of leadership or another, which afford us the opportunity to be a hidden observer. You can view these screen renditions to put into complete context the qualities of leadership that will be discussed. You can even replay the selected scenes to test the observations that have been offered in the book and hopefully to develop some of your own.

At the end of your time at the movies, you can determine how you stack up against these depictions and map out your own plan for self-improvement that focuses on the qualities that are most needed to elevate you to the next level. You can also use these films to enhance your understanding of your subordinates, your superiors and your colleagues. This is a serious treatment, but one which is meant to be fun and entertaining at the same time. It is also intended to sharpen your acuity in the observation of leadership skills.

You and your performance are observed every day by the people that you work for, the people that work for you, the people you work with and, indeed, people outside of your company. Like it or not, there is a constant rating of your talents. Put yourself in the position of the various characters described in this text. Under the circumstances portrayed in the film, how would you behave? There are lessons to be learned, and I hope that you take those lessons to heart and use them to help you make the most of your leadership performance.

As I said when this chapter began, the secret is that there is no secret. The qualities which make up great leaders are fairly obvious. In my teaching of successful, proven leaders, I have challenged them to name those qualities they most associate with leadership. Every class came up with what amounted to the same twenty or so qualities. The most significant of those are the ones that will be addressed in the chapters that follow.

The films and the characters portrayed in them have been selected because they succinctly dramatize one or more of the qualities necessary for successful leaders. I make no apology for my selection of films. My intention is simply to use the movies selected as examples to stimulate your appetite and sharpen your skills for the observation of the qualities of leadership. As I have said elsewhere, you are highly encouraged to seek out the films and view them in their entirety. The scenes I have identified and ones that you may identify on your own will hopefully become fodder for discussion with your colleagues, your friends or your family members. Put your feet up, grab the popcorn, and enjoy the show!

PATTON
Core Values

"Old Blood and Guts"

Few opening scenes are more impressive or have more of an impact than that in *Patton*. George C. Scott ascends the stage, dwarfed by a huge American flag, and gives an incredibly inspiring, emotional and dramatic speech to an unseen audience of U.S. soldiers. The speech, replete with colorful language, disparagement of the Nazi enemy and praise for the U.S. military, aptly captures the style of this near-mythic figure, "Old blood and guts," at his apex. The speech is rough, it is transparent in its patriotic verve, and it reflects General Patton's core values.

Like most military biographies, this stylized biography of General George Patton abounds with leadership lessons as it depicts the protagonist's heroics. Patton is the antithesis of the unassuming hero, Sergeant York, in his approach to life and his leadership style. He believes he has been chosen by powers beyond this earth to lead men in battle in great wars.

The film portrays the life of Patton from his exploits in North Africa to his death in Europe shortly after the war ends in 1945. It recounts the glory of his actions but also provides an accounting of some of the many controversies in which he became embroiled during his leadership tenure. While he was a highly decorated hero and a brilliant military tactician, he displayed an ego that, even for a general, was over the top. From his predilection for flamboyant uniforms of his own design to his pearl-handled pistols, he was a picture of narcissism. The film explores Patton's deep belief in reincarnation and his preoccupation with his personal destiny as well. In sum, this motion picture is a relatively straightforward chronological presentation of Patton's highly-documented activities during World War II.

The Foundation of His Style

An early scene that we will explore lays the foundation for what we are to learn of Patton's style. It is a relatively short segment, but it provides the opportunity to observe several qualities of leadership. Hopefully the description here will give you enough information to understand those qualities and at the same time whet your appetite for a viewing, probably not your first, of the scene and the complete movie.

As the scene in question unfolds, we see Patton arriving at the site of a battle that has just been concluded. Tanks, jeeps, equipment of every type and dead bodies are strewn as far as the camera can pan. Middle Eastern peasants are desecrating the still warm bodies, stripping them of boots, jackets and valuables. In all, it is a horrific panorama. After chasing off the peasants, the coterie of soldiers that had accompanied Patton goes on to his new headquarters to replace the commander responsible for the defeat just witnessed, and Patton is seen speaking to his aide. "You know why these men lost?" he asks. "They don't look like soldiers, they don't act like soldiers, and they're scared." Patton pauses, lights his cigar and announces, "In about fifteen minutes we're going to change all that. They're going to lose their fear of the Germans, because I'm gonna give them something to be fearful about."

The scene fades, and another one in the officers' mess hall, fades in. Patton strides in with his usual imposing look. He is spit-shined from his boots to his helmet. He has his ever-present pearl-handled revolvers strapped to his hips, and a leather riding crop tightly held under one arm is firmly grasped in his right hand. His aide follows. The cook welcomes the general in a casual way and inquires as to whether or not he wants some breakfast. By his words and his manner, Patton leaves no doubt as to who is now in command. "Am I to understand that all of the officers have not eaten yet?" he asks sharply. The cook looks surprised and responds, "Well, hell, General, it's only eight thirty, sir. Most of the officers don't come in till around nine."

During this interchange, two disheveled officers appear in the doorway. Patton hardly glances at them, and directing his continued attention to the cook says, "Please inform these officers that the mess hall is closed. From now on you will open at six a.m., and no one will be admitted after six fifteen." The cook acquiesces with a "Yes, sir." Then Patton goes on. "Where are your leggings?" With a quizzical look the cook responds, "Leggings? Sir, I'm a cook!" Patton glares at him and announces for all to hear, "You're a soldier!" The General then turns to his aide and orders, "Any man who is caught out of uniform will be skinned!" But Patton is not finished with his rounds.

Much to the amazement of its inhabitants, the General makes his way through the enlisted men's barracks. After looking around, he stops at a revealing pin-up posted at the foot of one of the bunks. Using his riding crop, Patton slashes the paper poster from the wall with an announcement that, "This is a U.S. Army barracks, and it is not a French bordello!" Still not finished, Patton next appears in the field hospital where he shows that he came by his nickname of "old blood and guts" honestly. He takes in the general scene and peruses a clipboard with apparent lists of injuries and treatments. The attending physician awaits his attention. "Doctor, am I to understand that you have a case here of battle fatigue?" "Yes we do General" comes the physician's reply. "Well," barks Patton, "get him out of here. He doesn't belong in the same room with these brave men." A shocked doctor counters, "But, General, he cannot recover unless we treat him here." The doctor is met with a cold stare and a colder response: "I don't care if he dies, just get him out of here!" With that, the General begins to exit and then returns his attention to the doctor. "Where is your helmet, doctor?" With a smug look on his face, the doctor parries, "I can't use my stethoscope if I wear a helmet general." Patton smiles and directs the man, "Well, doctor, have two holes cut in your helmet so you can."

This series of short scenes offers a world of insight into many of the qualities of leadership. But before taking an in-depth look at the central quality, there is value in looking at some of the others depicted in this scene, rich as it is with the stuff of leadership.

The Power of Example

There are many truisms concerning leadership, but none is more fundamental than the rule that it is best to lead by example. The days of the paternalistic "Do as I say and not as I do" approach to life in the workplace are long since over. The new generation of employees is more demanding of mentors and superiors, expecting to be given reasons for what they do and to have the active participation of men and women at the top in the tasks that need to be done. There is more admiration for the leader that directs, "Let's go!" and less for the old-style boss who exhorted, while looking down on the battle, "Charge!" The military, however, even as it evolves, continues to rely very much on the "Do as I say" approach, especially during times of war. The very fact that Patton had stars on his shoulder and guns on his hip gave him all he needed to command. He didn't need to have his subordinates "buy in" to his vision.

Yet, it would be a mistake to be dismissive of Patton's leadership example because today's leaders do not have the same luxury of leading by dictum. You may not find that to be a luxury at all and may even consider it to be a repugnant form of leadership. Whatever your views on Patton's style of leadership, try to look beyond the style and glean the significant lessons which are offered.

Although he was of a different generation and his environment was one in which he could, and was even expected to, lead by command and not consensus, this hero was always careful to lead by example; he might even be the epitome of this quality. Leaders of all types and in all disciplines would do well to do the same. Patton teaches us that it starts with the fundamentals. His look, his demeanor, his gait, his attitude, all bespeak the approach he expects from others, an approach that is evident in several scenes in the film. It is worth a synopsis of each.

When Patton's convoy is held up by a peasant and his stubborn donkeys that are blocking a vital bridge link, the General dismounts from his jeep and jogs to the bridge and takes action. Much to the horror of animal lovers around the world, he pulls out his pistol, shoots the offending animals and orders them thrown off the bridge to clear the way. Later, when confronted by gridlock, he again gets out of his vehicle and personally directs traffic to break the jam. All of the observers of this action are in awe of his hands-on approach.

All great leaders know something about leading by example, but seeing it played out in all of its cinematic glory brings the quality to life and lets us see how forceful it can be. There is probably no better character to illustrate this quality, since leading by example was Patton's forte.

Empowerment Equals Power

Recall the scene described earlier in which the bedraggled officers enter the mess hall and Patton does not address them but addresses the cook instead. "Inform these officers..." This offers another significant lesson on leadership, a quintessential example of empowerment, a nuance that should not be missed. Patton could easily have informed the officers directly. But, instead, he chooses to send the message that this was the cook's mess hall. Without saying so, Patton gave the cook the responsibility for his domain, and, more importantly, he made the cook accountable for results. All leaders know that responsibility and accountability go hand in glove, but seeing it here leaves a much stronger impression than words of instruction alone.

In almost every utterance in the scenes described, Patton is delivering messages and providing a wealth of leadership examples. With brevity and clarity, he lets his expectations—and the consequences of not meeting them—be known. There is never any ambiguity in his messages. One of my former Westinghouse leaders used to say, "Let me make this crystal g**d*** clear"; he practiced the Patton method.

This is another important lesson for leaders, who must take care that the messages they send are not convoluted or subject to interpretation. The recipients of a leader's message should not be looking for the hidden meaning. As emphasized in the opening chapter, all leaders and those that would be leaders are being observed. Every action, every word of an organization's leader sends a message, intended or not. The messages delivered by Patton in these scenes are, of course, intended. They are specifically designed to deliver one overarching message, among others: there is new leadership, and things will be different. Patton's messages are even intended to convey how the new leadership will be different. Watching the scenes leaves no doubt as to what he is trying to say about what he expects and what will happen if someone falls short. More importantly, Patton unveils his core values in these short scenes, and that is the quality that will be explored in greater depth in the remainder of this chapter.

Core Values Develop Over Time

In the opening chapter, homage was paid to the fact that we are all the sum of our accumulated knowledge and experiences. It is that accumulation that helps us to develop our core values; those core values will, in turn, form a foundation upon which each person's individual leadership approach is constructed.

The movie version of Patton's life does not spend any time delving into the recesses of Patton's past to unearth the causes and effects of his particular values system. The film does touch on his belief in reincarnation. And letters to his wife reveal some of the thoughts about what drives him in his quest for victory. But we are left without much information about how Patton's values evolved and developed. There is little doubt, however, about what those core values are and how they manifest themselves in his role as leader of one of the most remarkable war efforts in history.

Likewise, it is important for each of us to understand our own core values and how they influence what we do when we lead. We are being observed and listened to, and we are sending messages whether we mean to do so or not. There is not much room for debate about whether Patton's messages were intended. His early line—"In fifteen minutes these boys will lose their fear of the Germans"—is telling. With these simple words, Patton has set out his vision and established his purpose. He also gives his view about why the battle was lost in clear language. "They don't look like soldiers, and they don't act like soldiers." The statement is full of unmistakable messages about the importance of looking and acting like a soldier, and in later scenes he tells those around him something about how he thinks a soldier should look and act.

The message is always reinforced by Patton himself who personifies a professional warrior. Spit-shined, crisp, confident and clear, he *is* that soldier, he is a warrior, someone he values above all else. After the scene in the mess hall, it is unlikely that the cook or any of the others had any question about what Patton meant, about what he was expecting and about what would likely befall any of the men who failed to perform as expected. The importance of sending a clear, strong message about what you expect and what is important to you cannot be overstated, and if you want your message to be understood and accepted you will need to be sure that you "walk the talk."

A message, like the one in the opening scene, should leave little room for misinterpretation. The values meant to be conveyed in later scenes were more complex, more esoteric; and although the men knew what the commander was saying, it might have required more deliberation and thought from them—and us—to decipher what was behind some of his orders. The scene with the pin-up in the barracks seems most banal at first glance, but reflection suggests that there is more to Patton's behavior than meets the eye. "This is a barracks and not a bordello," he says. Did that mean that he was taking a moral stand against prostitution? That no woman would be allowed to be displayed? That no non-military postings would be allowed? Or was it just that he was taking the opportunity to take command and issue an edict that would send a message that things were going to be different? It was a rare utterance that would be up for interpretation. Even so, any of the potential interpretations left no doubt as to who was in command and that things would be different.

The scene that goes furthest in unearthing the depth and the nature of Patton's core values is in the hospital. "I don't care if he dies" is a profound statement of Patton's disdain for anyone or anything that does not exhibit the West Point core values that are embodied in its motto: Duty, Honor, Country. These are the things that are at the heart of Patton's system of values. In letting the doctor know that he thinks that the battle-fatigued soldier violates these principles, Patton at the same time is letting the rest of the injured men know that he thinks that they uphold those principles that he holds dear. Our protagonist's message for the injured is, "I honor you for your sacrifice, and we are in this fight together." He is also telling the medical staff, "I do not agree with the notion of battle fatigue or anything of that ilk. I will check for myself, and I expect you to follow my orders on this matter."

His order about the helmet sends yet another message: "You are first a soldier and then a doctor. You answer to me first and then to Hippocrates." In all of this, Patton's most basic message, and one which he consistently adhered to during his army tenure, was that he would not be sensitive to, nor would be he abide by, requirements of political correctness.

The ability to communicate core values is one key to any leader's success. Of course, a leader must first have sincerely-held core values to communicate. Self-professed leaders who adopt the core value du jour will soon be found out. Core values need to be real, since they will have to provide shelter if you find yourself in a storm of controversy and provide comfort at times of defeat. Core values are what you are really about, not something you came upon by putting a wind sock outside your office to determine what might be the most popular approach for the day. Core values are just that, they are at your core, and all behavior emanates from that core. In this regard, the commentary following the recent death of Pope John Paul II is worth noting. There was always controversy surrounding his pronouncements and his conservative views on matters of faith and human conduct, and yet there were universal expressions of admiration for his resoluteness and the consistency of his values in the comments made on his life.

Delivering the Message

You may not aspire to be like the Pope or like Patton, but you cannot expect to achieve excellence as a leader without consistent performance emanating from fundamental values. If you don't use 'em you lose 'em. Having very strong and well-defined values but not communicating them or having a purported set of values that you don't apply to yourself is worthless. You don't have to wear your values on your sleeve or even communicate them verbally. But to succeed as a leader you do have to have your actions be a reflection of your values. The most successful leaders are those who are known for their core values without ever having articulated them, whose actions bespeak their values.

This film tells the tale of a character that, in many ways, sets a standard of leadership, and you can measure yourself against that standard. Many of the lessons of leadership in *Patton* are clear and unambiguous; others are more subtle and require more effort to uncover.

Thanks to modern electronics, you can watch the film and then replay the portions that you think can offer some leadership quality that is worth your study. You should measure yourself against those qualities since those around you, even if they never saw *Patton*, will certainly do so.

Be sure, in particular, to cull out and watch those scenes that provide opportunities to learn about message delivery. You will count scores of messages delivered by Patton, who seems never to miss an opportunity to teach by word or deed. Like it or not, you deliver messages every day as well. As all leaders, you deliver some message every time you are with other people within your organization. Whether you're walking in the halls, running a meeting or participating in a negotiation, even if you don't think that anyone is watching, your mood and your body language, as well as your words, will tell people something.

You need to use these opportunities wisely, and be sure that the messages being delivered are the ones that you desire to send. It is well worth your effort to give some thought to what those messages should be; then you can set about sending them forthrightly. Patton had great confidence in his own core values and in the messages he was sending when he said, "I don't care if he dies, just get him out of here." Notwithstanding the crude harshness of the declaration, it is a confidence and a deliberateness of message that anyone wanting to be a leader would do well to develop.

GANDHI
Respect

"A Man of Respect"

Mohandas Gandhi was a leader of mythic proportion. None of his contemporaries, not Winston Churchill, Franklin Roosevelt, Joseph Stalin, Adolph Hitler or Emperor Hirohito, could lay claim to the adoration heaped upon him. Although these other men dominated the world scene during the 1930's and 1940's, they did not stir the passions of their followers and enemies as Gandhi did. It was Gandhi, a slight man, humbly adorned in the most modest of cloth and shod with the bare essentials, who almost single-handedly changed the face of a nation. Indeed, he laid the foundation for changing the face of the world.

During the first third of the twentieth century, Britannia was no longer ruling the waves without challenge. England was losing its grip, some have said its stranglehold, on its vast empire as Africa, the Middle East and the sub-continent of India were experiencing the stirrings of nationalism. The middle class began to form and grow, and the paternalistic nations of England, France and Portugal began to realize that more resources would be required to control their far-flung territories that they had handled with such ease in the past. Historian Eric Hoffer described the fertile setting of the evolution of Gandhi as hero: "When government policies or historical accidents make the attainment of individual self-respect difficult, the nationalist spirit of the people becomes more ardent and extreme." Gandhi was both the product and the personification of the rise of the middle class in India.

The bio-epic *Gandhi* is a rendition of the life of Mohandas Gandhi. It chronicles his life from the time he was a young, somewhat naïve, lawyer until his public death at the hand of a lone assassin. It aptly depicts his metamorphosis from a practical professional with respect for British authority to a missionary of sorts whose vision compels him to assume the unofficial leadership of a nation.

A catalogue of the qualities of leadership exemplified by Gandhi would encompass nearly every quality exhibited by the finest leaders. Some of the qualities we associate with him include inspiration, vision, determination, focus, commitment, humility and integrity. These same qualities, however, can be seen in other leaders and in other films. The quality that most exemplifies Gandhi in this film and most sets him apart from other leaders is respect.

Respect is a quality which is fundamental in successful leaders. Voltaire captured this quality centuries ago when he wrote, "I don't agree with what you say but I will defend to the death your right to say it." This is an expression of respect for others but also imparts the notion of self-respect, and I believe the two are inexorably linked. The notion of respect goes well beyond just tolerating others and what they profess. The notion of self-respect transcends self-esteem or self-image and includes respect for one's own core values and how those values present themselves in human interaction.

Self-respect can manifest itself in complex life situations and in the most mundane of circumstances. The youngster growing up in the ghetto—or, in today's vernacular, in "the hood"—who walks tall and tries to find the right path rather than blindly mirroring the behavior of his peers can be said to have self-respect. In a world far away, the corporate type who refuses the questionable perk from a vendor can be said to be driven by self-respect. And the woman striving to break the glass ceiling who displays disdain for off-color remarks is also displaying self-respect. When we see people who have self-respect, we might describe them as being centered, at peace with themselves, or comfortable in their own skin. But whatever description we choose, we recognize self-respect as an essential ingredient in every successful pursuit.

Self-respect is difficult to measure, but, like the tone set by Patton in the earlier chapter, it is the bedrock of success, as is so movingly demonstrated by Gandhi. It is a characteristic that he often outwardly displays through dignity. In fact, he was ever, and above all else, dignified. Dictionary definitions of dignity include poise, stateliness, reserve in deportment and the very trait under consideration, self-respect. Gandhi's picture could have been next to any of these definitions. The leader who has a high degree of self-esteem and who can naturally carry that over into respect for others is the leader who is prepared to succeed.

Respect Is Not a Choice

No leader I have ever studied was more sincere in his respect for his detractors or even his sworn enemies than Gandhi. It was his self-esteem that led to his respect for foe and friend alike. Gandhi had a certain regard for those who opposed his vision, and that regard was founded upon his respect for himself. In point of fact, he showed reverence for all things and all people.

Although the movie about Gandhi's life is suitably lengthy given his monumental accomplishments, the lessons to be learned from him about respect are best depicted in a couple of brief scenes. In the first, at the beginning of the film, Gandhi, recently admitted to the bar, suffers the pain and humiliation of discrimination at the hands of an overzealous train conductor who unceremoniously throws him from the moving train upon Gandhi's refusal to exit the first class compartment for which he has a legitimate ticket. Even as he suffers this indignity, Gandhi remains dignified. This is the beginning of a revelation and the transformation of the soft-spoken professional, who thus begins the journey to lead his people on a radical but nonviolent attack on the English and their occupation of India.

As the movie unfolds, we see Gandhi's association with other Indian leaders, his acts of defiance and the speeches he delivers to mixed reviews to his Indian audiences. In all cases, Gandhi quietly drives home the inviolate premise of non-violence, the tenet probably most strongly associated with him. At one meeting, Gandhi declares that he is willing to die for a particular principle but not willing to spill one drop of another's blood or take another's life for that principle. On more than one occasion, he is jailed for his protests.

The background of another scene where the quality of respect takes center stage is one that depicts Gandhi, knowing full well that only his native countrymen did any meaningful work in India, leading a successful effort to have Indians boycott all labor. The effort virtually shuts down the country. Of course, the British are appalled at the prospect of having to carry their own bags or drive themselves to the market or train station, and Gandhi's leadership role in the boycott results in his arrest and ultimate incarceration. At his public trial, when the judge offers to release him upon payment of a small fine, Gandhi refuses so that he can make his point by serving his sentence. The judge trumps Gandhi's effort by releasing him anyway, thus denying his attempt at self-sacrifice. Undaunted, Gandhi ends up imprisoned for yet another labor strike.

This key scene opens with Gandhi and his fellow prisoners queuing up for the midday meal in the open yard of the prison, holding out bowls to be filled with a porridge-like concoction. Like everyone else, Gandhi is clothed in a shabby prison uniform with a prison number emblazoned on his chest. He is engaged in hushed conversation with a friend, when he is interrupted by a guard who informs him that the commandant of the prison demands his presence in the commandant's office.

Gandhi follows the guard and is escorted to an opulent office suite. He quickly makes himself as presentable as possible by brushing the dust from his tattered garb and assuming an erect posture and confident countenance. The commandant has his back to the diminutive prisoner and is pouring a drink from a well-stocked bar tray. Turning toward Gandhi, he inquires, "Would you care for a brandy?" The reply is a curt, "No, thank you." Nodding toward an appetizing tray of meats and cheeses, the commandant further inquires, "Would you care for something to eat?" Gandhi, remaining stoic, quietly replies with great dignity, "I dined at the prison."

Even When No One Is Looking

In that moment in time, our hero makes a huge statement about his respect for self. We can also conclude from this scene that he is delivering many messages. He can be said to be adhering to the combat dictum: Ask no quarter, and give no quarter. He can be said to be displaying the adherence to his mantra of self-discipline. He may also have been declaring that he was not subject to bribery, even though choosing to eat or drink would not have compromised his positions in any way. He could have taken advantage of the situation by accepting nourishment to ensure his strength for the challenges ahead. He could even have satisfied his hunger without the possibility that his followers would ever find out about his momentary lapse in discipline. He chose self-respect instead. Self-respect is, among other things, doing the right thing when no one is looking and when there is no chance of exposure. No single moment on celluloid better portrays this quality than this scene.

But the incident is just the beginning of a scene that is richer still in lessons about respect. As the scene continues, the two men seat themselves opposite one another at the grand desk of the British officer. The commandant begins the conversation by reviewing why Gandhi is in prison and the state of the present situation in India.

In earlier scenes, the audience has witnessed the leadership of Gandhi. He called for a general labor strike as a result of a very oppressive set of laws imposed by the British government. The laws included the right of the British to enter the homes of Indians without cause and to pursue a variety of intrusive actions meant to demoralize and bow the Indian people. These laws crystallized Gandhi's thinking and set the stage for his eventual leadership of the Indian people. The labor strike initiated by Gandhi was very successful, and his imprisonment did not hinder its continuance. The British now recognized that they had to deal with this substantial man. With this as a backdrop, the British officer confronts Gandhi, gingerly suggesting that perhaps he can influence the commission that is being formed to review the new laws. This begins an unannounced negotiation between the two leaders. Gandhi's subtle facial expressions, captured on film, portray his surprise and quiet delight in realizing his people are on the verge of victory. With no excitement in his voice, he compliments the officer by conceding that the officer's influence would certainly result in a change. Here, he displays respect for the leadership of his host and deep respect for the fact that he has influence well beyond the prison. The two men have now become equal despite their slave/master relationship at the meeting.

The commandant goes on to explain that he, of course, can not guarantee that the commission will accept a member from the Indian people. As he explains this, he makes it clear through his expression that he is asking Gandhi, "Will you insist on having Indian representation?" Our hero gives a lengthy pause, considering his response. Finally, he explains, "We did not contemplate this commission before calling the strike, we wanted the laws suspended." He goes on with his very careful wording, "I do not see why, just because we are in a position of advantage, we should expand our objective." Together the two men reach agreement, and the officer offers immediate release to Gandhi. After boldly borrowing enough money for train fare from a shocked British underling, Gandhi bids farewell to the commandant and begins to depart. When the underling moves forward to escort him, Gandhi straightens to his full height and announces, "I can find my own way out, thank you."

Equal Footing

It is worth exploring what this scene subtly but vividly depicts. From the time Gandhi enters the room, he never assumes a subordinate position. His entire demeanor suggests equality. His self-respect is personified in every aspect of his actions. All of us have experienced similar circumstances. Who among us has not been in the position of being the "low man on the totem pole"? The point of this scene is to never behave like the low man or, of even greater moment, never to feel like the low man. This is not to say that it's not important to respect authority and the chain of command; but you can maintain your dignity while being respectful of rank, proffer due respect while retaining confidence in your personal worth. Put another way, when in the company of superiors in rank, you need not give in to a belief that you are among superiors in character.

The scene is stark in its depiction of Gandhi as having achieved a great victory against the British government. There is no question that the strike has brought the occupiers to their knees. Yet, even in victory, our hero, great leader that he is, never gloats.

And there is more to be learned from taking a closer look at the interplay between Gandhi and the commandant. When the officer queries his guest as to whether or not there will be insistence on Indian representation on the commission to review the laws, Gandhi pauses thoughtfully. He can respond in several ways. Recognizing that victory is his, Gandhi senses that he can win an additional point by pressing his advantage and demanding Indian representation, but his respect for his opponent comes into play at that moment. Gandhi chooses not to insist and, more significantly, he explains his logic. In effect, he says that the intent of the strike was specifically to suspend the laws and that any new or additional demands would be morally wrong.

In this way, Gandhi not only is true to himself but proclaims that he is a fair man who will not take advantage of his opponents.

He gets the victory he was seeking but allows his opponent to save face. It is truly a powerful display of the role that respect can play.

Relationships Are Connected to Process

This is a great lesson to negotiators at all levels. Leadership is not a one-time event. Leadership is a process. Leaders know that relationships are more closely connected to process than to outcomes. As a popular catchphrase advises, "What goes around comes around." Gandhi intuitively knew the value of allowing the opponent to end a negotiation gracefully before it was de rigueur. We have all witnessed aspiring leaders who squeeze the last ounce of blood from the opponent or subordinates. The actions of these would-be leaders and their casting of the world in terms of victory and defeat are destined to retard their efforts to lead. Respect for others demands that you leave an avenue for dignified retreat.

The actions in this scene are remarkable for their subtlety as well as their power. The messages are clear but require insight and study. Like many of the other lessons in cinema, they rely on the expressions and the demeanor of the players. Gandhi's exit, for example, is brilliant in its delivery of message. He uses few words when declaring, "I can find my own way out." Left unsaid is the more significant message, "I am no longer a prisoner; I do not need an escort. I am an equal, and I follow no one. I lead."

Toward the end of the film, Gandhi is portrayed as having emerged and matured as the recognized leader of his people. He is seen in his handmade, unadorned wraps of white cotton which he has adopted as yet another message to his people and to the British. By this stage of the story, he is seen at the center of a conference table flanked by his colleagues; across the table are the

British leaders, and the discussion centers on the future of India and its governance. It is obvious that at this juncture Gandhi is viewed by both sides of the table as the spokesperson of the Indian people and one who has earned grudging respect from the occupiers of his country. The scene is noteworthy. He has won every major skirmish with the British, and he has a great deal of real and residual power; yet, he is still controlled, quiet, dignified and respectful.

As this particular scene unfolds, the leader of the British contingent is speaking of how it might be necessary to adjust some governance issues in the future. He gives verbal recognition to excesses of the past and appears to be prepared to loosen the reins a bit on the Indian people. He does, however, make some remarks that are reminiscent of the earlier British superiority. When the arrogance returns, Gandhi cuts off further discussion by introducing the notion that the time is approaching when the British will have to leave. As the camera pans the table, shock, dismay and incredulity are on the faces of the British. Those around the table cannot believe the temerity of the man. Finally, one of them girds himself and, with practiced British understatement, inquires, "What would you expect us to do...just leave?" All eyes are on Gandhi when he says, with some finality in his voice, "Yes. Just leave... Just walk out." The shock deepens in the usually imperturbable Brits.

Then another man appears in the camera lens. He is wearing a smirk with a born-of-British arrogance. The uniformed general, his voice dripping in sarcasm, says, "You can't believe that the Indian people are capable of governing themselves. Utter chaos would result. Who would administer the country?" With an understanding nod indicating that he is considering the source of the comment, Gandhi retorts, "We would prefer being in chaos while governing ourselves rather than being ruled by unwanted occupiers." Now with everyone's undivided attention, Gandhi proclaims the obvious, that "A hundred thousand British can no longer rule millions of Indians if they do not wish to be ruled." The gauntlet has been thrown.

In this meeting, Gandhi assumed clear command. Inherent in his pronouncement was his intent to ensure, through his personal leadership, that his people were prepared to make that statement a reality. This sets the stage for the eventual bloodless coup. The occupation ends, as Gandhi prognosticated, with the British just leaving. The departure of the British was with pomp, circumstance and ceremonial flourishes, but they nonetheless just left.

During the conference scene, never once did Gandhi declare victory, never once did he ridicule, never once did he threaten, and never once did he raise his voice. The scene was a microcosm of his adult life and a synopsis of his leadership style. He was ever the man of respect. He was resolute in his beliefs and wore them on his sleeve. During his undeniable quest for the freedom of the Indian people, he never compromised his principles.

Gandhi built a foundation of self-respect but recognized the necessity to respect others. Most people strive to gain the respect of others. Those same people often fail to recognize that respect is a vehicle on a two-way road. Respect for others needs to be in direct proportion to respect for oneself, and Mohandas Gandhi is an unquestionable example of both.

4 *12 ANGRY MEN*
Judgment

"Judge Not, Lest Ye Be Judged"

Technology has always had a great impact on human interaction. Witness the ubiquitous cellular phone, check your wireless E-mail, or use an MP3, and you need no further evidence of the impact of technological advances on our lives today. Motion pictures, too, have been the recipients of the marvels of technology. Films without color are now "art films." If there are not spectacular chase scenes, pyrotechnic extravaganzas or unexplainable gratuitous special effects, there is little hope of a box-office bonanza. We have come to measure success in films by the cost of the effort. Such was not the case in the 1950's.

In the fifties, an overwhelming majority of films were in black and white, and few had special effects. A notable exception was the very expensive *The Ten Commandments*, which was in blazing Technicolor and was renowned for the spectacular parting of the Red Sea brought to us by Moses. (Incidentally, this simple trick photography was accomplished by running upside down motion pictures of Niagara Falls reversed against each other.) High tech to very low tech, *12 Angry Men* is the opposite of *The Ten Commandments*. Yet, this low budget classic remains memorable for its studies in leadership qualities and challenges. *12 Angry Men* is a simple film that should be viewed by all who profess to be students of human interaction or leadership.

While technology has transformed virtually every aspect of society, the American jury system, which is the subject of this movie made and set in 1957, has remained virtually unchanged. Technology has certainly invaded the courtroom, but the fundamentals of the jury system are essentially the same as they were at their inception. The same can be said of all the qualities of leadership. Technology has not had any impact on the traits associated with leaders.

12 Angry Men's depiction of a jury in action is distinguished by its sparse setting and mono-scene backdrop. Save for less than five minutes that includes the opening scene and the closing scene, the entire film unfolds in the jury room and attached men's room of a county courthouse in New York City. It is set on what is described as "the hottest day of the year" and in a room without conditioned air. The twelve white male jurors have convened to reach judgment on an eighteen-year-old Hispanic who is being tried for the murder of his father. All of the men have sport or suit jackets and some have ties, all of which add to the heat of the day. The stifling atmosphere in the room is palpable.

Following instructions by the judge, the jurors retire to the deliberation room and, after some shuffling around, are called to order by the foreman. There is some banter before it is suggested that they take an initial tally to see where they stand. Asked for a show of hands, eleven of the men raise their hands to show they favor a guilty verdict and, almost in unison, they stare at the lone dissenter, played by Henry Fonda. Without much of an outward expression, he has raised his hand in support of a not-guilty verdict. The reality of being alone in his dissent is stark. It is obvious that the other men are in disbelief at his judgment.

The entire movie has one ongoing primary plot about sitting in judgment in the American jurisprudence tradition. There are many subplots which are played out as the story unfolds as well. Many leadership qualities are portrayed in this film, but the one this chapter will focus on is judgment. *The American Heritage Dictionary* provides one definition which is apropos: "The ability to form an opinion by distinguishing and evaluating." Successful leaders must possess and exhibit sound judgment.

The Foundation of Leadership

Sound judgment is another one of those qualities which is difficult to measure, but it is at the root of a leader's effectiveness. Judgment does not depend solely on knowledge or the collection of data. William Penn put it most succinctly when he said that, "Knowledge is the treasure, but judgment the treasurer of a wise man. He that has more knowledge than judgment is made for another man's use more than his own." In the context of a jury trial, each juror embarks on the deliberations with more or less the same knowledge of the case at hand. Each member of the jury has been exposed to the very same testimony, opening and closing arguments, judge's rulings on objections and, of course, the judge's instructions. The jurors can be said to have the same knowledge about the subject before them. With this equality of knowledge, *12 Angry Men* begins to unfold.

Since the film is essentially one continuous scene, the production is brilliant in the way the camera occasionally focuses on a pair or a threesome of jurors having some interaction. In this way, the audience begins to see and hear the various preconceptions and viewpoints on some of the minds that are already implacably made up. The sole dissenter hears one such man proclaim, "These lawyers talk and talk even when it's an open and shut case." When the protagonist bucks the tide by casting his vote for "not guilty," several in the room ask him to explain his position as if they cannot possibly understand how a right-minded person could reach such a conclusion. By his reply—"I don't know, I want to talk it through"—the holdout makes it clear that he is not committed to any decision but rather is just not yet prepared to say that the teen is guilty.

When the dissenter begins to talk about the youth's troubled past, another man, whom we could rightfully refer to as "the bigot," talks about how "they" are born liars and he has lived among "them" and you can't trust "them." In turn, each juror takes time to summarize his position in an effort to convince the lone wolf.

Time and again when confronted with the facts that were presented, including eyewitness testimony, and his logic is questioned, the juror all the others are trying to convince replies by calmly saying, "It's possible." He continues to talk about the accused and his background. He explains that he cannot vote for guilt without exploring other views and possibilities. He proclaims that such a weighty decision, which could result in death for the young man, requires some deliberation and discussion. After a time, the dissenter announces that although he is not sure, he will yield to the decision of the group. He says that if all eleven of his detractors vote affirmatively for guilt on a secret ballot, he will abide by that decision and vote for the boy's guilt as well. When the secret ballot votes are counted, one more person votes for acquittal, and the contest for the hearts and minds of the rest commences.

At this point, the dictionary definition of judgment is played out as the hero begins to distinguish and evaluate. At the same time, the ten remaining guilty voters begin to reveal their styles, approaches, personalities and prejudices. We observe that, in addition to the bigot, one is a loudmouth, one a bully, and yet another is a wise guy. There is a self-absorbed intellect, a working man, and gradations of all of these. When the intellect lays out a very logical progression of the evidence that should convince any rational man, the hero listens intently. Each time arguments are made, he listens with equal attentiveness. Leaders should learn from this behavior.

Listen First

It is impossible to develop sound judgment without superb listening skills. A successful leader needs to hear and understand every aspect of any argument which impacts a decision. In watching this film, one can readily observe the central character as he absorbs the arguments of others. Following absorption, he then addresses each argument in logical sequence and counters or questions the conclusions that have been drawn. He does so without rancor or ridicule. At strategic moments, he even appears to agree with some of the arguments that have been made by the others. When asked, "Do you think that the accuser's lawyer wouldn't have been smart enough to ask that question?" he responds by saying simply, "It's possible, it's possible." He never admits logical defeat and always leaves room for further exploration. But first he listens. Sound judgment requires good listening.

In a very dramatic segment, Mr. Intellect, supported by Mr. Bully, says confidently that he finds it impossible to believe that a very unique knife (the murder weapon) was lost by the accused and somehow was found and used by the murderer. They call the bailiff to deliver the knife to demonstrate the point that the knife was unique in its markings, and the bully sinks the knife into the table to dramatize the argument. The hero suggests that there may be other knives like this one, but Mr. Intellect scoffs and declares that such a possibility is non-existent. With this, the hero rises to the height of Mr. Intellect and produces an identical knife which he, also with great drama, sticks into the table next to its twin. Amidst the many gasps of surprise, he explains that he was out walking in the neighborhood and easily purchased the knife for a couple of dollars.

A leader not only listens but, like the hero, senses the appropriate time to respond. Often a leader is a counter-puncher rather than an attacker. A leader accumulates necessary data, assesses situations in full context and makes judgments based on that data and those assessments.

Again, the definition of judgment as "the ability to form an opinion by distinguishing and evaluating" applies. As events unfold, the audience witnesses the Fonda character carefully observing and listening to sidebar discussions and comments. Aspiring leaders should carefully observe him as he constantly weighs the timing of opportunities to achieve his goal of convincing the others of the existence of reasonable doubt.

A leader engages and disengages at strategic moments, using his judgment to weigh whether or not the moment is right to advance his goal. When Fonda senses, through careful observation, that the timing is right, he directly confronts a potential defector by asking, "What do you think?" He never fails to win a new ally when he uses this tactic. He also never asks one of the hard cases an opinion, because his judgment tells him that such an inquiry would only provide an opportunity for the other juror to further rant about the guilt of the young accused.

Quiet Leadership

There is much to be learned from the Fonda character in addition to his unimpeachable judgment. He is dignified, professional in his demeanor, steady in the face of attack and direct in his approach to his fellow jurors. He is what I call the quiet leader. This film should be studied by leaders for many reasons, which we will continue to explore, but mostly because there is a popular belief that a leader is the inspiring person at the head of the pack who exhorts all the others to do better and to do more. Leaders are often thought to be those who take charge in a confident or even self-important manner. This approach often draws others to the leader or to the cause. That's just not the case with Fonda's character, whose quiet leadership makes him every bit as effective as someone more outgoing or forceful might be in the same situation.

This character has to listen intently to formulate and deliver counter-arguments, he has to labor hard to convince others, he has to remain calm and logical, and he has to apply strategy to a set of circumstances in an effort to bring others across to his point of view. It is clear from the beginning of the film that he has not made a final judgment as to guilt or innocence at the conclusion of the trial, and he is aware that the process of persuading others to allow for an open mind is not going to be an intellectual battle alone. As an architect, he possesses an orderly mind and relies on precision, but he remains open to arguments based on emotion or bias. The audience witnesses the rising confidence in the hero as he formulates his own conclusion, while measuring the content of the opposing arguments. There is leadership art in his actions. He succeeds without bombast, without a loss of integrity and without compromising his values. He is, as noted, a quiet leader who should serve as an inspiration to any leader whose personality is well-suited to this style of leadership.

The hero demonstrates also that to be quiet is not to be bland. The purchase of the duplicate knife is a testament to his innovativeness and creativity and his ability to spark a reaction in others. Early in the discussions, after the bigot refers derogatorily to "them," the hero takes the first opportunity to mock the bigot and his reference. By so doing, he puts everyone on notice that he may be mild-mannered and polite, but he won't run from a fight or refuse to confront those who tread on his values.

When the bully continues to intimidate and confront, the Fonda character—for the most part—ignores him. The hero allows others to take on the blowhard, for example; when he shouts most disrespectfully to the old man on the jury, the "working man" comes to the old man's defense. In these instances, this leader appears to stand back, not because of cowardice but because of judgment. In his judgment, timing is all-important in confronting the most visible of the opposition.

In similar fashion, the bully, in an early confrontation, trumpets the fact that the accused threatened his father the night of the murder, in fact threatened to kill him. When the Fonda character suggests that threats are often made without any intention to carry them out, he is loudly mocked by the bully, but the hero chooses not to engage further in the confrontation and allows the subject of conversation to change. Later, when the discussion of the threat is forgotten, the hero judges that the time is ripe to spring his trap.

Following a particularly violent verbal outburst by the bully, the hero pounces with a response borne of increasing confidence. "What are you some kind of sadist? You want to pull the switch yourself?" The bully is now growing visibly more inflamed and beginning to physically move toward the hero. The Fonda character continues without pause, "You are really sick, just sick." With the last words the bully rushes at the hero in a rage and fails to get to him only because several jurists grab him and hold him back. The bully is shaking his fist and screaming, "I'll kill him, I'll kill him!" Calmly, and without retreating an inch, the hero says, "You don't really mean you'll kill me, do you?" This was the perfect rejoinder delivered at the perfect time. As the camera pans the room, it is clear that the impact on the individual jurors was not insignificant. The bully's credibility was destroyed just when he seemed to be gaining support for his guilty vote. Counter-punching at its best worked magic.

In many ways, this film is a microcosm of challenges which leaders of every ilk face. Viewers can easily identify the various personalities and the difficulties in dealing with each of them that are part of the hero's challenge. In fact, it's necessary in watching the film to associate each juror with a personality trait since surnames are never used in the film until the final scene outside the courthouse. The film is both subtle and brutally direct. Some lessons, such as that embodied in the soliloquy delivered by the bigot, are crisp. Other lessons are more by way of nuance, as in the flip-flopping of the man in the grey flannel suit. Few films can lay claim to so many messages in such a simple setting, and yet the star is a complex study in leadership success that deserves repetitive viewing.

Convincing the other jurors one by one, this quiet leader transforms the eleven from a group united in favor of a guilty verdict into a unanimous voice in favor of acquittal. He does this with sound judgment at every turn. The entire film is a study in leadership and in human interaction. Leaders can learn much from the actions of the protagonist, and many of the lessons are timeless: Counter-punching can be more devastating than initiating contact. Bigotry clouds judgment. Truth is not always apparent. Silence can be a potent weapon. Non-confrontation is not weakness. Timing is as important as knowledge. Allies are not always recognizable. Sound judgment is a force multiplier.

Consensus Is a Force Multiplier

Socrates lends his name to, and thus gets the credit for, the questioning methodology of great teachers. Great leaders often emulate this great Greek by posing questions that require some thoughtful consideration to answer. It is a powerful tool, since questions force thought. In this vein, the hero here constantly asks thought-provoking questions. Through these probing questions, he forces his fellow jurors to think and defend their positions. When challenged to defend his own position, he resorts to a statement which begs another question, "It's possible, it's possible." This prompts the question, "Is it? Is it?" Eventually, all twelve angry man agree that it is, after all, possible.

The entire film deals directly with consensus-building in the classic sense. Today's work environment requires consensus-building. As noted in the discussion of *Patton,* gone are the days of dictates. Like the Baby Boomers and the X'ers, the future corps of employees will be mobile and agile. They will have many choices and few allegiances. The lessons in *12 Angry Men* will serve leaders well in dealing with this future workforce.

5 SEABISCUIT
Determination

"A Horse Is a Horse, of Course, of Course"

Sports and sporting events have always provided opportunities to observe leadership traits and qualities played out under the watchful eye of the public. The boxer exhibiting courage in the ring, the football coach strategizing from the sidelines and the point guard marshalling his forces on the basketball court, all provide a window of opportunity to see leadership in action. There have been scores of cinematic efforts that take us inside the locker room and the dugout for a bird's-eye view of the motivations and rationales of the players being portrayed. Sport undeniably provides a rich reservoir of leadership qualities, but few portrayals are more poignant than the one that is the subject of this chapter.

In 1938, the second- and third-most-written-about figures in the United States press were Franklin Roosevelt and Adolph Hitler. The most chronicled celebrity turned out not to be a person but a horse. Seabiscuit was the central character in the most optimistic story of the mid-1930's. The successful motion picture, *Seabiscuit*, was based on a book of the same name and used an historical backdrop as dramatic as the film itself. This was a time when the nation was in the midst of the great depression. The unemployment rate exceeded 25 percent, and the depression was as surely psychological as it was economic. The entire nation was in a deep funk and in desperate need of a tonic that would relieve the symptoms, if not the disease. The story of Seabiscuit became that elixir.

The film rendition of the *Seabiscuit* book was far more than a chronicle of the wins and losses of a remarkable animal. The film, to be sure, is about the horse and his exploits, but it is equally about the three men who were enriched by their association with the equine hero. In fact, any description of this horse could also be a metaphor for any of the other central figures in the story.

In contrast to other films explored in this book, *Seabiscuit* offers lessons given by an ensemble cast. A raft of leadership-conducive traits are possessed by the actors: honesty, passion, vision, compassion and optimism among them. It is of value to understand the "baggage" each carries in order to understand the one trait they share.

Looks Aren't Everything

Seabiscuit was never a splendid looking thoroughbred, quite to the contrary. The typical athlete who runs the race in the sport of kings is tall, broad-chested, high-spirited and slender of leg. In fact, the father of Seabiscuit, Hard Tack, did cut such a figure; and Seabiscuit's grandfather, Man-o-War, could be the prototype for thoroughbred horses. But this was not so of the offspring and grandson. No, Seabiscuit was a small horse with short legs, one of which flailed sideways when he galloped, and his breath came only with a wheeze. He was like a perennial teenager in that he valued sleeping and eating much more than running. To describe his temperament as cantankerous would be kind. All of the foregoing notwithstanding, his lineage made him a thoroughbred by definition.

Seabiscuit, this runt of the litter, was destined to track the life of most horses with pure bloodlines. He was bred to run and was ordained to travel the exasperating road of the racing life.

Those who had an early hand in his training had no patience for his attitude and slovenly work ethic. He was relegated to the role of "lead pony" for those horses with better credentials and smoother proportions, not to mention ready speed. When Seabiscuit was entered in races, they were usually of the variety known as "claiming races." These were races in which the horses were subject to be claimed, literally, by anyone willing to put up a predetermined price, which was the purse of the race. Seabiscuit was a ne'er-do-well who was perceived as a marginal contributor in the world of horse racing. Before he became associated with the caretakers that would change his life, he had lost his previous seventeen races. Seabiscuit was a loser.

A Unique Collection of People, Each With Strengths

Jack Pollock, who would come to play a pivotal role in the evolving story of Seabiscuit, was possessed of a body that was not designed to mount and race thoroughbreds. The model jockey was short of stature, rarely weighing more than 105 pounds and never more than 114. Red was around five-foot-six and had to literally starve himself to get to less than 120 pounds. He had a mean temper which often led him to be quick with his hands, many times at the peril of those who angered him. If you were trying to imagine the stereotypical angry redhead, you might conjure up Red Pollock. One might suggest that he was a "human Seabiscuit."

Red was abandoned by his mother and father to a roust-about promoter of informal horse races, this in an effort to increase the survival potential of the parents as well as the son. Red was devastated by the desertion of his parents, but he loved the animals and the itinerant racing life. It suited his temperament and his competitive nature. Still, Red Pollock achieved no fame and no real success as a jockey and was eventually let go by his niggardly boss/guardian because he did not win often enough. Red was a loser.

Tom Smith, who would also play a very large part in the ultimate story, might be known as a horse whisperer. He had been around the beasts most of his long adult life. He had been a trainer of race horses, although with an undistinguished record. Tom was a humble, modest man who, until the time of the serendipitous meeting-up with Seabiscuit, had every reason to be both modest and humble.

Despite his lack of success until then, Tom did have a special way with the magnificent animals that were his charges. He would often save a horse from sure destruction by assuming ownership of an injured horse just before a bullet was about to "put the animal down." Through the very patient tending and coaching they received, the horses that Tom took in often survived and thrived because of his special gifts. Yet, none of his talent resulted in wealth. On the contrary, he was unable to hold on to any meaningful employment and was sometimes unable to even afford food for himself because he had only enough to provide for his adopted project horses. In the eyes of many, Tom was a loser.

Charles Howard, another of the fascinating cast of characters here, was a man of means. He was a transplanted Easterner. When Horace Greeley exhorted all to "Go west young man, go west," Howard listened. In fact, Howard succeeded and accumulated wealth well beyond the dreams of most. He did it through hard work, ingenuity, an optimistic outlook and the willingness to take risks in the business world. His car dealerships spun off sufficient cash to afford him, his wife and his adored pre-teen son all that wealth could provide. In the time of the late 20's and early 30's when a quick wit and some capital could erase any limits on success, Charles Howard, with his sharp mind and charismatic personality had it all...and then came the depression.

The Great Depression had a huge impact on the entire world and on each of the key characters in *Seabiscuit*. The wealth accumulated by Mr. Howard was not immune to negative impact, although it was not entirely dissipated like the fortunes of so many then. Howard suffered reversals and was forced to drastically cut back on his lavish lifestyle, but he was far luckier than most in his ability to continue to enjoy an existence that was not bereft of the finer things in life. He was not so lucky, though, in his family life. His young son, whom he idolized, was tragically killed in an accident while driving one of the family vehicles. Years away from eligibility for a license, the son took an adventuresome and ill-fated drive while his father was away on business. The boy could hardly see above the steering wheel. Howard, of course, was devastated by the tragedy, and the calamity was compounded when his wife left him in his emotionally-wounded condition. After a while, Howard sought solace in travel to Mexico, the company of a sympathetic female soul mate and horse racing. He very much thought of himself as a loser.

At the confluence of all of these histories, the four characters are brought together in Mexico, each having arrived as broken, or at least damaged, losers. The title of an old Sinatra song may say it best: "Here's to the losers, bless them all."

As it turns out, three of these down-on-their luck individuals—Howard, Pollock and White—come together because of a fourth, Seabiscuit. Howard, who always was enamored of racing and was looking for a diversion from his depression, began to think of owning a thoroughbred. While in search of prospects, Howard comes upon an older gentleman caring for a hobbled horse using unconventional means and asks the old-timer if the horse can race. The man answers in the negative, and Howard further inquires as to why, then, he's fixing him. The man, Thomas White, tells him, "Because I can." After a bit of thought, White continues, "Just because he's beat up a little, ain't no cause to throw a whole life away." This lesson, once laid bare, will figure time and again in the story of the movie.

By Any Other Name

Persistence is the leadership quality or trait which is best captured by this film. It is a trait that each of these heroes can claim as his own. Some might call it tenacity or determination; others would probably call it stubbornness. But by whatever name it is known, it is the ability to optimistically continue in the face of adversity or doubt. The scene just described shows the trait in perhaps its most simplistic form. There are a number of other scenes that show us more about the value of persistence.

While pacing around the paddocks and tracks, Howard comes upon Seabiscuit who gets his attention by being disruptive with everyone who approaches him. Howard and Tom like his spunk. Howard's business sense tells him he can own the horse for the low claiming price, and he becomes a new owner with an old trainer and a cantankerous horse. The trainer and owner move on in search of a jockey. Once they observe the pugnacious Pollock in his most confrontational state, they can easily envision a team of misfits: the frenetic Charles, the volatile Red, and the Zen-like Tom.

Together, the unlikely trio proceeds to turn the fortunes of the little horse around. Seabiscuit thrives under the tutelage of Tom and the gentle hand of Red. In the process, first the racing public and then the general public take notice. The story of Seabiscuit presents a microcosm of a nation that is looking for a symbol of hope for those who are down but not quite out. Mr. Howard contributes mightily with promotional genius which magnifies "the biscuit's" successes. When asked by a rabid press corps what turned the horse around, Howard alludes to the entire country when he announces, "We gave him a chance, a lot of people out there know what we're talking about. That is what turned him around, just giving him a chance." The mass media, looking for its own way to turn itself around, is riveted on the exploits of Seabiscuit.

Bent Is Not Broken

Seabiscuit embarks on an incredible winning streak. In a major race during his remarkable winning streak, Seabiscuit loses by a nose. Speed was not the issue; rather, when Pollock fails to see an approaching horse on his right, the knowledge comes too late for adjustment. The nation seems stunned. When berated by Tom, Red reluctantly admits that he is blind in his right eye. The flabbergasted old trainer sadly informs Charles Howard and concludes that they will have to change jockeys. While recognizing the risk associated with saddling a one-eyed jockey, Howard shows his true grit when he uses Tom's fateful words from the past to express his disagreement: "Just because a life is banged up a little ain't no reason to throw it away." The admonishment is not lost on the trainer, and the determination colored by loyalty that the scene portrays catches the audience in its grasp. The team remains together. It is still later in the film when the determination of the team will be put to its most rigorous test.

The four central characters continue to contribute to victory after victory. The whole country, hungry for a cause which will divert it from real hunger, embraces the little horse that could. As news stories further enhancing Seabiscuit's latest feats abound, everyone is clamoring for a head-to-head duel with the reining eastern steed of the era, War Admiral. Of course it was Howard, ever the promoter, who continued to fuel the flames of the thirst for the competition by taunting the owner of War Admiral. After many aborted attempts, a face-off race was finally scheduled at Maryland's famed Pimlico race track. It was estimated that 40 million Americans—one in every eight people in the country—tuned in to hear the call of the race. The little horse that could...did. For a brief time the rigors of the depression were drowned out by the hoof beats of a winner

The very next race, again followed by millions, brought tragic results. Seabiscuit came up lame. The prognosis was grim, and the track vet suggested putting the game little horse down. But Charles Howard would have none of it, and the three men brought the horse home to live out its hobbled days. During the horse's convalescence, tragedy struck again when Pollock was dragged crashing into and through a barn while still attached to the saddle of a horse he was riding. His leg was so shattered that he was told that he might never walk again. Of course, he was warned never to ride again, should he ever recover enough to even walk. The horse and jockey shared the same fate, and the greatest test of determination was about to begin.

Red and the Biscuit hobbled together. Day by day, they could put more and more weight on the injured limbs. There came a time when Pollock could put a homemade splint on his boot which allowed him to sit astride Seabiscuit and walk the horse gently around the stable area. Biscuit began to trot and eventually to gallop. Soon whispers of a potential race could not be ignored. The only challenge remaining for the legend was the Santa Anita Derby, the race he had lost because of Pollock's impaired vision. Unfortunately, by this time Seabiscuit was seven years old and would have to face the finest three-year-olds, in the prime of their lives as race horses. The only ally of the aging and injured horse was determination.

Red Pollock was a different story. He and Howard had been told that he could lose the use of his leg if he ever had even a minor spill. But when Red hears the rumors of the Santa Anita race, he comes to the track and confronts Howard, who is at the time conferring with George Wolf, the most famous jockey of the era. Howard berates Pollock for considering the ride in Santa Anita, saying, "You could be crippled for the rest of your life. I won't have it!" Red screams back at him, "I was a cripple until he made me better!" Wolf enters the confrontation with the thought that it is "Better to break a man's leg than his heart." The outcome is better than any amount of sentimental yearning for a Rocky-like ending could have created. The reality is that Seabiscuit with Red Pollock aboard won the Santa Anita Derby, with thousands of onlookers screaming with excitement and millions more listening to their radios in astonishment.

There could scarcely be a better story to showcase the sheer determination, the dogged persistence that is a significant aspect of good leadership. Each of the prime players in this movie exudes this leadership quality, although it is interesting to note that each of the central figures is motivated in his determination by something different. Still it is determination that is the cornerstone of the success of each one of them.

Power In Persistence

Tom White was determined to rely on his own special skills and not to yield to the methods of the day when training this unique steed. White's was a tenacity motivated by quiet confidence in his own abilities that prompted him to resist what he saw as training trends and novelties.

Aspiring leaders can certainly take a lesson away from all of this. It is easy to fall prey to the current thinking about good leadership styles and waver in your determination to lead in the way that uses your strongest skills. Indecision about whether to follow your own path or to go with some popular leadership fad is often a curse created by a lack of confidence. Leaders know that confidence, borne of a lot of hard work and good judgment, is the foundation of determination.

Of all of the leads in this film, Red Pollock could be characterized as the least centered and the most fragile. His particular brand of determination teetered on the brink of stubbornness. Stubbornness is tenacity out of control. Red was so determined to be a jockey that he regularly starved himself to make the required weight. He was determined, often only by force of will, to regain enough strength to attain his vision of riding Seabiscuit to victory in the Santa Anita, even if it risked permanent crippling. Pollock was an overachiever who knew that he could find the path to success through persistence, often marked by sacrifice. He was fortunate to have the others to smooth the rough edges and funnel his volatility until it became a controlled flame that fired his success.

Charles Howard drew his tenacity from a dogged optimism. His catchphrase in the film, "To the future," summed up his life perspective. He was a self-made man who knew the virtue of hard work and the value of creating a vision. There are probably no examples of great leaders who were not optimists, and Howard was optimism itself. He was always optimistic as he worked with determination to extract maximum performance from each of the contributors. Perhaps none of these unlikely heroes could be described as leaders, at least not in the classic sense, but the most likely candidate is Howard because he comes the closest to being the glue that binds all the others together.

Dig For What Lies Within

Finally, of course, there is the lead character, Seabiscuit. Bred to be a leader at the track, Seabiscuit had all of the blood lines of the leading racers but required the right set of circumstances to bring his talents to the fore. This may be the most compelling leadership lesson of the film. Like Seabiscuit, few of us know the qualities of leadership that lurk beneath the surface. Perhaps circumstance alone is the trigger, or maybe it's the inspiration of others which brings forth these qualities, sometimes spontaneously. Think of the many tales of heroism you've heard from Medal of Honor winners who have no explanation for their outbursts of leadership and self-sacrifice. We all have within ourselves the qualities of leadership. Events can bring them to the surface, or we can work to nurture them and hone them through hard work, using our own determination to accomplish our personal and business goals. Most importantly, when qualities of leadership surface, embrace them and apply them.

Charles Howard, Tom Smith, Red Pollock and Seabiscuit all embraced their own determination and tenacity and used them to get where they were going. As a leader, you will—like all of these characters—face adversity in achieving your vision or completing your project. You can look to this film to capture the essence and the virtue of persistence. As a leader, you cannot allow challenge or obstacles to stop you in your tracks. You must anticipate adversity and steel yourself against it with determination if you are to lead. For example, when building a project budget you build in contingency, which is all about anticipating and preparing for difficulties that may arise. Building in contingency is a tool that helps you to be persistent by paving the way to overcome those difficulties.

The force of your own will and your own personality are also tools that can help you to remain determined. Preparation and passion, too, are allies of persistence. When does persistence become stubbornness? Successful leaders learn to sense the difference between the two. Watch the characters in the film and you will see times when determination has at least the potential for becoming stubbornness. You can witness this dangerous phenomenon and avoid crossing that line yourself.

In the final analysis of this film, the lives of the prime players are so intertwined that it is difficult to determine who had a greater impact on whom. Upon being complimented on taking a broken-down old horse and making him a winner, Red Pollock had an insightful observation when he responded by saying that, "We didn't fix him, he fixed us." It was determination that helped them all get well.

ERIN BROCKOVICH
Preparation

"The Boy Scouts Are Right"

Can you recall when you were so well prepared for an action or activity that you were the picture of confidence? There is no feeling quite like the sense that your whole being is silently crying out, "Bring it on, give me your best shot!" It can be before a big test in college or in a sporting event in which you are competing or before a meeting with your boss. But whatever the occasion, what a joyous feeling it is! Experience, knowledge, instinct, comprehension, awareness and skill, to name a few of the elements at work, all contribute to being thoroughly prepared. Preparation is not an art, it is a science, one that is required of all leaders. Preparation is the opposite of flying by the seat of your pants.

Many films, some included in this book, portray a protagonist who is prepared for leadership. In the case of military people, we correctly assume that they have undergone the rigors of some academy or other and come up through the ranks to take command. In other cases, we are led to believe that the central figures somehow earned the positions they hold.

Few films do a better job of showing preparation at work than *Erin Brockovich*. Erin Brockovich is a real person, and the film portrays the events in her life which have made her somewhat of a heroic figure in some venues. Erin, a woman of limited education who is struggling with the trials and tribulations of everyday life, is a single mother whose accomplishments in life are few and whose surroundings are extremely modest as a consequence when we meet her.

At this time, the seminal event in Erin's humdrum life is having lived adjacent to a chemical plant which uses toxins in its production processes. The effluents and wastes that are discharged by the plant have always been regarded as a part of production, a way of doing business. But there is a growing suspicion that those byproducts may have played some role in various illnesses that have been contracted by neighbors of the plant. Through a series of happenstances and circumstances, Erin begins to formulate a hypothesis that there is a direct correlation between the activities of the plant, owned by a corporate giant, and the illnesses, suffered by the unassuming townsfolk. Although her early inquiries are met with skepticism, Erin's notion that the plant is causing medical problems gains increasing support from the empirical data she gathers, which bolsters her own strong intuition.

Through tenacity and sheer willpower, Erin convinces a modest one-man law firm to take up the battle against the corporate giant. The middle-aged lawyer/owner is emboldened by her passion, enthusiasm and work ethic. He is taken with her cause and adopts it as his own. In league with one another, they set about building, brick by brick, a case that will prove to have significant legal and moral implications.

The often overwhelming task of gathering the data for the case is tedious and painstaking. Day after day and week after week, we see Erin tracking down the potential victims of the environmental travesty she is attempting to expose and interviewing them to extract their rendition of life near the site and the details of the medical and emotional impacts on them. The viewers are caught up in the dedication of Erin, who seems to be oblivious to discomfort as she perspires in trailer homes, compassionately convincing the "victims" to unburden themselves of their stories and emotions. For many, it is a cathartic experience.

In addition to the countless families Erin must interview and catalogue, she is also seen fighting the various bureaucracies she must contact and question in her attempt to establish links which are crucial to her case. She is seen in all her street-smart glory as she uses her womanly guile and charms to gain the attention of potential suppliers of information. The audience goes back and forth—at times caring about this character, even lionizing her, but at times repulsed by her foul-mouthed, thug-like approach. In all situations, she is consistently unrelenting. Her education about the case and general preparation is meticulously comprehensive.

Competence Equals Confidence

There is a single scene which most vividly extols the virtues of preparation. The lawyer whom she has enlisted to join her efforts gradually comes to realize that they have, indeed, uncovered facts that will allow them to connect the dots and directly establish the parent corporation's culpability. Unbeknownst to Erin, he seeks the assistance of a major law firm specializing in class action torts of this nature. He invites two of that firm's experts, a man and a woman, to a meeting with him and Erin to review the state of the case thus far developed. The meeting is depicted in a scene that is rife with tension.

In a large but unadorned conference room, the camera unveils Erin and her boss sitting on one side of the table, the male member of the expert team at the head of the table and his female cohort standing beside a large file folder box on the other side of the table in front of the white board. The female expert appears to be preparing a presentation of some kind. Erin's boss introduces the pair as experts from the big city, and Erin's reaction, her "attitude," is unambiguous. Her facial expressions suggest surprise and concern, and there is anger building. If the word "blindsided" could be portrayed by an expression, it would be the one on Erin's face at this meeting.

It is worth your while to see the film, perhaps not for the first time, to carefully observe Erin's posture and expressions for yourself. As promised in chapter one, you do not have to be a fly on the wall in Jack Welch's office to get up close and personal with lessons in leadership—you just have to go to the movies. Looking at a particular movie to examine a particular leadership quality in depth is a way to become that fly. This scene embodies that notion. In the meantime, let's return together to the scene to get an idea of what can be learned.

The female expert opens the dialogue noting, "We have gone through some of the files and find them interesting." Erin cuts her off with a question, "Are those my files?" with the emphasis on "my." "Why, yes," comes the reply with the additional comment, "You have done some very good research here and when we fill in the holes I think we have the makings of a case." Erin straightens her back or, better put, gets her back up and says, "There are no holes in my research." There can be no mistaking the tension in the room. The camera pans the faces of the men, and their expressions alone speak volumes as the scene unfolds. The male expert's countenance silently says, "Wow, do we have a spunky one here!"; while the boss, well aware of Erin's volatility of which he has on occasion been the target, appears to be thinking, "Look out, she's about to blow." A pregnant pause blankets the conference room.

The attorney engaged in the exchange with Erin patronizingly says, "I think you have a very good start here, it's just that we have to fill in the blanks." Erin replies with undisguised disgust, "Don't talk down to me lady, I may not have gone to college but I know more about this case than you'll ever know." Another pause, punctuated with the tension, reverberates in the room.

The expert, familiar with confrontation, backs off, choosing the valor of discretion and says, "Well, we will need things like phone numbers, and some addresses are missing and things like that is what I meant." If Erin could get her back up any higher, she does so upon hearing this and exclaims, with that now hot attitude flashing, "What numbers do you want?" The expert assumes an expression of disbelief as she retorts, "You can't tell me that you have memorized all six hundred of the phone numbers of the people in these files." Without uttering a word, Erin strikes a pose that uses her body language to say, in no uncertain terms, "Go ahead, test me." Getting the message, the expert rifles through the folders, extracting one and opening it and asks, "Annabelle Daniel?" Erin begins a very lengthy reply. It includes the complete phone number and then the precise address.

With little hesitation, she goes in for the kill. She expounds with great detail concerning the medical condition of the girl and all her relatives who lived in the same proximity of the plant. She drives the stake deeper by talking in detail about the victim's recreational habits and her ambitions. The rendition includes a variety of proclivities and other assorted details intended to drive home the personal relationship Erin has developed with her clients. She continues with chapter and verse before concluding by bringing up several other names and asking, "Do you want their numbers and diseases?" Smugness replaces anger in her countenance.

Again, the camera pans the faces of the male lawyers, one of whom shows resignation while the other shows anticipation. The female expert, sensing defeat now embraces discretion as a significantly better part of valor. "Perhaps we have gotten off on the wrong foot here." Erin, disposing of any modicum of diplomacy spits back in retort, "That's right, lady, that's all you have is two left feet and f***ing ugly shoes!"

A Message Both Eloquent and Clear

In this relatively short scene filmed in a Spartan-like conference room, there are volumes to be learned about one of the most critical qualities of leadership: preparation. No more time and no additional money spent on the set for this scene could have made the simple but eloquent message any clearer. There is no substitute—neither courage, nor intellect, nor passion, nor wit—for preparing oneself for the challenge at hand. It is a powerful lesson that is powerfully shown by a woman who, by hard work alone, has obtained and mastered all of the available information from all possible sources.

The result, and a central theme of this movie, is the triumph of the weak and the meek. It's in the spirit of *The Grapes of Wrath* set in a more modern world. The scene, in the context of leadership, is mostly about work ethic and pure preparation, teaching us that they are at the heart of most successes.

Beyond what is obvious, the film and the particular scene that has been described contain nuances about the process of preparation. For example, Erin was fully prepared emotionally to connect to the victims by virtue of the fact that she had shared their lifestyle. She had physically prepared for the laborious work of hoofing about in the heat and the discomfort of unconditioned air in homes similar to her own. She may be an underdog, but in her tenacity and ability to endure she is like a bulldog, and it is difficult not to root for her as she strives to achieve her mission. Erin overcomes what might be viewed as insurmountable obstacles with the power of preparation. Erin represents the "lowly" undereducated minority, rising to gaze into the highly-educated, successful eyes of her intellectual superiors without fear or doubt. With the benefit of complete preparation, she levels the playing field. Preparation can thus be the great equalizer. It's something the boy scouts have long recognized as an asset: be prepared. In this, the boy scouts were right.

Leader, Manager or Lone Wolf?

Is Erin a leader? She certainly possesses many of the qualities of leadership. She communicates effectively to those with whom she needs to relate. She is committed to her goals and has a vision of where she wants to go. She is creative and intuitive and can inspire when the occasion requires. Does the mere possession of many of the qualities of a leader translate into being a leader? The answer, of course, is no. In fact, in the final analysis, Erin is more a manager than a leader. In the workplace, she might even be characterized as an outstanding individual contributor. She displays no ability as a team player, no ability to adhere to procedures, no sensitivity for hierarchy or chain of command or process.

She is more comfortable as a lone wolf, a renegade. She constantly exhibits an unrestrained "attitude" which comes to the fore in the scene in the conference room. When you view the entire film, you are likely to admire what she did and how she succeeded, but you would not likely want her working for you. Most assuredly, you might be uncomfortable in having her lead, without surveillance, a major complex project. All of that said, the scene which displays her methodical preparation is a brilliant cinematic vignette about that quality.

In a sense, the scene shows us that a quality can have the vices of its virtues. We cannot help but applaud the knowledge of the facts that underpins Erin's confidence, and yet most students of leadership would recoil at the attitude that is borne of the same confidence. Is Erin a heroine and villain in the same scene? Her attitude problem is, in part, caused by her background as well as her passion, but her boss's mishandling of the situation also contributes largely to her unprofessional behavior. He blindsides her by bringing in support without consulting her or even warning her, as a result of which she is defensive from the outset of the meeting. Her boss was responsible to communicate his vision of a winning strategy and thereby enlist her support for the litigation experts who could help her achieve her vision of succeeding for her clients. As a leader, her boss failed, and Erin is made to look overly aggressive and crude as a result. But with all of her failings as a leader, the value of her preparation is never in doubt.

Like many people all of us know, Erin may not be a leader but does possess many qualities of leadership. Leadership is something more than just this quality or that one, which is probably why millions of words have been written on leadership but nothing contains the secrets on how to be a leader. The intent of this book is to present an opportunity to concentrate on the individual qualities of leadership and to provide each reader with dramatized depictions which can be used to study the particular quality that is played out in the drama. In the case of *Erin Brockovich*, the depiction is enhanced, as it is so often is, by the main character's body language and expressions.

If the scene described is read or heard without the benefit of seeing the body language or those expressions, it might not offer that same lesson on leadership or provide the same insights into Erin's personality or skill and the use that she is able to make of her impeccable preparation. The scene without the expressions and body language would be akin to listening to the lyrics of a song but without the musical accompaniment.

Leaders need to hone the quality of thorough preparation. Like all leadership qualities, this one alone does not a leader make. But without preparation, a leader opens the door to luck, something that, by definition, no one is able to control. Preparation minimizes the luck factor. We have all heard from or about the leader who modestly lays his or her success at the doorstep of luck, but the very smart guy who once quipped that accomplishment is one percent inspiration and ninety-nine percent perspiration probably came closer to the truth. Prepare to succeed, or open the door to failure. You owe it to those whom you lead to be prepared to the greatest extent possible for that leadership.

Paralysis Through Analysis

Like many leadership qualities, preparation can be carried too far. Preparedness can be overdone when the analysis of the facts stands in the way of taking action. There are leaders who never "pull the trigger," characterized, as a result, as indecisive by their subordinates and other observers. Without question, the inability to make timely decisions can be a fatal flaw in leaders. These unsuccessful leaders worship at the altar of preparation, preparation and more preparation. They need just one more study, one more piece of data, one more survey or one more opinion. In the meantime, the battle is lost; the window of opportunity has closed, and the door of failure has opened wide. The Patton quote concerning battle plan execution is as apropos here as it was in a preceding chapter.

Earlier, it was noted that preparation is a science and not an art. It is a skill that can be learned and honed. Yet there is an art to preparation which lies in knowing when the preparation has been sufficient to support a sound decision. The application of all the knowledge that has been accumulated through preparation is a high art indeed. Erin had all the information necessary to take on the high-priced lawyer from the big city. She was confident that she had prepared more than enough to prevail in the confrontation that evolved and that set the stage for her successful working relationship with the outside lawyer. It was the preparation that infused her with confidence. If you are to become a leader, you will need to be imbued with the same confidence which has as its wellspring preparation.

HIGH NOON
Ability to Inspire

"Lead, Follow or..."

The qualities of leadership are immutable. As man has gone from being hunter-gatherer to farmer to industrialist, leadership qualities have remained the same. Hollywood too has been steadfast; from the silent films to recent productions that are chock full of special effects, production companies continue to make movies with actors who exhibit the same basic qualities in the characters they portray.

In the early 50's, *High Noon* was a much-awarded motion picture, and Gary Cooper, its star, was winning critical acclaim for his performance as Sheriff Will Kane. It was a perfect role for Cooper, one that seemed to be made for him. Cooper epitomized the strong silent type, and Will was the quintessential strong silent type as well. The actor and the character have more than a few positive traits in common, but there is a real leadership surprise hidden inside this classic.

The film's essentials are fairly straightforward. While there are undercurrents of an imminent marriage and remnants of an earlier affair, the core of the film deals with the retirement of the successful lawman. Kane's retirement and planned exit from the community come at a precarious time in his and the town's life.

Will Kane initially donned the silver badge when the town was in turmoil, and he earned his coming retirement and his reputation during a turbulent tenure. Typical of many western towns of the late 19th century, the bullies and roustabouts ran roughshod over gentle townsfolk who were seeking a new life and a new start on the frontier. When Will became sheriff, he quickly focused on bringing the troublemakers to heel. The film is brilliant in establishing the sheriff's talent and character without going into the history or specifics of his successes; rather, we see the result, a placid community with a positive outlook that shows only gratitude for its savior. In this regard, *High Noon* is a far cry from the depiction in the popular HBO series, *Deadwood*, although the television version might be more accurate with respect to the coarse and violent ambiance of early western life.

An early scene quickly lays the groundwork for the film. The local telegraph operator is viewed in his railroad station office where he has transcribed a message with devastating news: Frank Morgan, the erstwhile leading town thug, is being released from prison and returning to town to extract his promised revenge. The message is directed to Morgan's partners in crime and includes an invitation for them to join the newly released prisoner in quenching his thirst for vengeance. The telegrapher wastes no time in informing the town hero of the plan of the gang, and the battle lines for the upcoming confrontation are drawn.

Kane receives the news and displays little emotion at the potentially explosive situation portended by Morgan's missive. Will owes no debt to anyone either real or perceived, and he has options. One of those options is to continue with his post-wedding plans and quietly ride off into the proverbial sunset. Exploring yet another option, he shares his dilemma with his deputy and tells his assistant that together they can organize and fight the good fight and win. His deputy quickly begins to backpedal, and,

finally, showing us that he is the antithesis of positive leadership, he abandons his mentor and hero. Left without the deputy's
support, Will settles on a strategy based on past experience and
courage. He determines that he will organize a posse and develop
and execute a plan that will reprise his past heroics and once again
save the town.

The next scene of import opens with the camera fading into
a view of the exterior of the ubiquitous country church, bathed
in white with a towering steeple. The church pulpit appears, with
the righteous preacher standing tall behind it and announcing the
theme for this Sunday morning. The church is full of the town's
citizens resplendent in their Sunday-go-to-meeting finery. As the
service begins, the doors of the church burst open, and we see Will
looking beseechingly at the Reverend. The Reverend responds by
inviting the sheriff to speak to the gathered faithful.

Will outlines the situation in some detail and explains
why he came to church on this day. He does so with the proper
solemnity and sense of urgency so that there is little doubt as to
the impending crisis, and then he concludes his soliloquy with an
urgent plea: "I'm going to need to deputize all the men I can get."
One of the men quickly replies, "Well, what are we waiting for?"
and, with that, a good number of men jump to their feet and begin
making their way to the center aisle. There is much murmuring
throughout the house of worship until another man stands to say,
"Hey this isn't our job. That's what we pay the sheriff for!" There
is an outburst in response, with some parishioners counseling the
others to join forces with the sheriff and some urging their fellow
townsfolk to let the sheriff take care of this on his own. There is
obvious passion all around as the chorus of voices in the church
reaches a crescendo. At last, one of the apparent leaders of the

community takes center stage. He gets everyone's attention and settles the session down. He then begins to conduct the meeting, calling in turn on each man who wants to have a say.

A Debate Followed By Failure

Will observes the flow of these events with his normal stoic posture, listening intently while the church members vent their views. One man, who clearly supports the lawman, extols his virtues: "This man made this town safe for our families. Most of us remember when Frank Morgan and his gang made it unsafe to leave our homes. Some people even left to seek a safer place to settle. Now that he needs our help, we have to give it to him." The roller coaster ride of emotions continues when the next man speaks up. "Not so fast. Why if Will had just arrested Frank's gang over the last couple of days we wouldn't be in this position. Why did he just let them roam around town waiting for Frank?" Like a ping-pong match, opinions on both sides of the issue continue to be bandied back and forth.

You may recall the importance of timing in an earlier chapter. Few characters are more adept at good timing than the emerging leader of the meeting. The townsman who assumed the chair and took charge of the meeting now commands the attention of the crowd. At this point, the prevailing view of the crowd is not clear, but it is evident that the groundswell of support for the sheriff that had been evident at one time is now receding.

The new leader now has the rapt attention of his audience. Putting his hand on Will's shoulder, the new leader now begins to speak saying, "Now I have known this man since he got to town. We all know what we owe him. We all know what he did for this town and that he deserves our respect and admiration." The self-appointed leader of the meeting pauses for effect and then continues, "It was he who put Frank away, and he is the one that Frank will want dead when he gets here on the noon train. Now as much as we owe this man and as much as I respect him for what he has done, I don't think Frank will do harm to others or to our town if Will just leaves. If Will is not here, there will be no trouble." In what is now a silent church, the new leader turns to Will and says with an air of finality, "Will, I think you ought to leave. I think that if you're not here when Frank gets here, he will not cause trouble. It'll be better for you, and it'll be better for us. " Will hardly changes his expression. He might be described as emotionally blank. With a few parting comments, Will leaves the church without having gotten any of the help that he asked for, without even the hint of a posse. Will Kane has failed in his mission.

Inspired Followers

Before moving on to the rest of the film, it is worth pausing to consider what happened here and to see what can be learned from the church scene. Will's qualities are clear. He is a man of integrity, courage and character, a proven performer with a track record of success. He is admired by his fellow citizens and held in some esteem as a pillar of the community. Yet, it is apparent that he lacks one essential quality of leadership—the ability to inspire others, which is critical to effectively lead. By definition, if no one is following, then you cannot be leading.

The dynamics of the situation in the church are certainly worth exploring, but it is worthwhile to first consider some of the differences between management and leadership that this scene illustrates. The ability to inspire is not a prerequisite for management, but it is a necessary element of leadership. For there to be a leader, there must be others involved, those who are being led. The same is not always true of a manager.

In some cases, a manager may manage people, and in those cases leadership is implicated; but managers can also manage things, such as projects or functions. The art of management infers control, measurement, documentation and other tasks which do not necessarily require leadership. Project managers simply do not have to be great leaders. It may be helpful, but it is not required for success. Project managers often have systems, procedures, technology and other tools to aid in their management of people and things, and it is those tools that are of most importance to their management job. Unlike a leader, a manager cannot rely on passion or vision or inspirational ability to get results. This is not to say that leaders should rely solely on passion or vision or ability to inspire, because that too can lead to failure. Rather, it is to say that the roles played by managers and by leaders are two very different things. With all of that in mind, we need to ask whether Will is an effective manager or an effective leader.

It is a question suggested in other situations as well. We have all heard, for example, about Notre Dame and Knute Rockne and the "Get this one for the Gipper" speech, and it is interesting to consider whether Rockne was using management or leadership. And when the President of the United States uses the "bully pulpit" to win support for his programs or position, is that a management or a leadership tactic? In looking at these and other instances, a good argument can be made that it is the ability to inspire that most often separates the successful executive from the ineffectual one. The ineffective leaders may have a plan. These leaders may also have adequate resources, and they may be superior in every measurable way. But if they cannot inspire those whom they lead—to adopt the vision, to take up the cause and to commit to get the job done—then they will fail.

The political landscape is strewn with leadership failures. Adlai Stevenson was a world-renowned intellect with major influence and stature. He ran for president twice while carrying the Democratic banner, the first time against Dwight Eisenhower. Almost since boyhood, Eisenhower had known no experience other than that of being a soldier. He had no formal political experience, and until one year before the election he had shown no political ambition. He had no known political philosophy. Indeed, until he declared for the nomination, he had no political affiliation. And yet all of the qualities brought to the table by Stevenson counted for naught when facing the war hero. All of the track record, all of the experience in public service, all of the intellectual superiority notwithstanding, Stevenson was soundly defeated, not once but twice. You can probably see some similarity between Will and Adlai; they were two huge talents who could not lead because they could not get anyone to follow. In both cases, the followers chose to follow someone else. In the final analysis, both men failed as leaders because they failed to inspire.

So with the benefit of some further thought on the matter, what happened at the church? Will went to the house of worship to muster some troops, but this effort failed. He had many admirable qualities to be sure, but Will's failure to inspire others caused him to fail at leadership. You can probably see by now that Will's reputation was built on being a good manager, not a good leader. He had been able to succeed over the bad guys and bring them to heel, but only after others identified the problem, set forth a vision and hired Will to bring that vision to reality. The town leaders hired a manager. It was as a manager and not as a leader that Will

Kane entered the Church. He was a manager looking for a tool, for a system, for a procedure...for unspecified help. He was the first to speak at the service and he laid out the situation with dispatch and calm; but he had made no very specific request by the time he paused for a response. He was not able to inspire the others by setting forth a vision or a game plan or sharing his expectations or his fear of the potential consequences of failing to act. He failed to lead. Will had no sense of timing and mistakenly believed that he need only explain the situation and request support. He not only failed to inspire, he created a vacuum in leadership. This happened because he committed a greater failure even than failure to articulate a strategy—he created a vacuum in leadership.

Leaders Emerge

When there is a vacuum in leadership, leaders fill it. The town father picked up the baton that Will dropped, and he filled that leadership vacuum in the church. By filling the vacuum, the town father became the leader, exhibiting many of a leader's qualities. He took control of the meeting. He established order ("Alright now, let's speak one at a time"), and then he called on the town's citizens as he saw fit. As he did all this, he listened attentively to each speaker and seemed to take note of the emotion contained in each expression of opinion, and then he chose the time that he would sum up the meeting. In his summation, he praised Will but laid out the consequences that might result from following Will's plan. He leads on by clearly articulating his own vision, the plan he thinks should be executed: "Will, I think you should go." The town father also envisions and voices why this is a good plan, saying, "It'll be better for you, and it'll be better for us." He doesn't take a vote or ask for any other opinions. And Will, with no other choice really, leaves defeated.

The story of Will Kane drives home the point of viewing the lessons in leadership dynamics in full context. The viewer can see the expressions on the faces of the players. Those expressions, or lack of them in Will's case, speak loud and clear. Will looks beaten before he is beaten, his entire demeanor that of a loser.

There may be an ethical problem with usurping leadership as the town father does, but that will be left to your own contemplation. Most viewers, in fact, do not find the man to be likeable. He is manipulative and opportunistic. You need not like him either, but you should strive to understand his leadership qualities.

The point here is the unmistakable demonstration of how vacuums in leadership are filled by leaders. The town father may or may not have been ethical or correct in his approach, but Will left a vacuum in leadership, and the town father filled it. With that, he turned the tide in his direction. He defeated Will, and ultimately Will conceded the battlefield to this new leader. Will Kane not only failed to inspire others, but he also failed to exhibit some of the most essential leadership qualities.

The Will Kane character in this film was universally considered to be a hero by those who viewed this classic. In fact, it is probably safe to say that any poll seeking to identify the most significant heroes and leaders among film characters from the last half of the 20th century would find *High Noon's* Sheriff Kane among those named. Despite being widely viewed in this way, a deeper look at his character presents a different picture.

What happens in the remainder of the film is romantic. Will watches the clock slowly tick to high noon and waits for what it, predictably, brings. Frank is met by his partners in crime, and they head to town to extract their pound of flesh. Single-handedly (almost), Will fights the good fight and, although wounded, he survives. The three bad men lay dead. Frank is killed, in the end, not by Will but by his bride, who as a Quaker is forbidden to use violence against another but who nonetheless kills her new husband's attacker. Good triumphs over evil. Will Kane prepares to leave town as the citizens come out from hiding to witness the carnage, and Will dramatically unpins his badge and throws it into the dirt on the street. Will's face reflects the disgust with which he regards the newly emboldened townspeople.

Admiration Is Not Leadership Success

As a manager of the resources at hand, Will was brilliantly successful. It is well worth watching the film with the thought in mind that there are layers to Will's personality. You will see a man we can all admire. We see someone who is loyal, trustworthy, candid and courageous. He has a proven track record of success and great experience. In his profession, he is at the top of his game. He is well-liked and respected by his peers and feared by his enemies. It seems that he could not help but be a leader. Still, all of his good qualities do not add up to leadership acumen. Whatever else can be said about Will Kane, he lacked a fundamental aspect of leadership without which he could not claim the title of leader.

It might be assumed that Will Kane's basic personality does not lend itself to inspiring others. As an introvert, he may not seem well-equipped to generate inspiration in others. But introversion is by no means inconsistent with the ability to inspire. You need look no further than Gandhi to be convinced that a quiet, soft-spoken individual can be profoundly inspirational. All leadership skills come in all personality types and sizes, but those skills must be studied and nurtured, and you need to make them work for you in your own personal way. Whether you are an introvert or an extrovert, understated or more bombastic, you need to find a way to inspire others with your own style.

The ability to inspire should not be confused with charisma. Charisma is, by definition, a rare quality attributed to those have demonstrated an exceptional ability for winning the devotion of large numbers of people. What it means to inspire is, by definition, to stimulate to creativity or action, to guide or to arouse. This is a much more humble, although far from easy, undertaking. You are born with charisma, or not; but, in any case, you can develop the skills to inspire. Later, we will return to the discussion of the development of leadership skills.

As for this skill, there are a variety of techniques to inspire others. Some inspire through fear, some through reward, still others through the use of surrogates. While there are many leaders and would-be leaders that are looked at in this book, no two of them use the same approach to inspiration. Study them all in the films that portray this particular quality, and observe other leaders around you for ideas on various techniques. When all is said and done, you will adopt the style with which you are most comfortable.

8 *LAWRENCE OF ARABIA*
Adaptability

"Going Native"

Thomas Edward Lawrence was a leadership enigma. He was a bastard child, a man few claimed to know intimately. His influence on the map of the Middle East is recognized by even his severest critics. He is mentioned in British military annals along with General Allenby, Lord Nelson and Field Marshall Montgomery. And yet, he is unfailingly characterized as somewhat of a screwball. He has been variously described as brilliant, insane, courageous, self-centered, focused, scatterbrained, godlike and demonic. He was, at best, a complicated man whose ability to lead was as much in spite of, as because of, his peculiar make-up.

The cinematic masterpiece *Lawrence of Arabia* attempts to put on film the exploits of T.E. Lawrence in the Middle East in the 1916 to 1918 time frame. The scope and splendor of the production were breathtaking for 1962, the year in which the film was originally released. The producers' ability to somehow bring a magnificent tapestry of color to what is arguably an extremely drab and monochromatic part of the planet is stunning. The cinematography and music alone would be worth the price of admission, but even those technical triumphs pale by comparison to the value of the biographical treatment of Lawrence himself. As in most bio-epics, the movie takes great latitude and theatrical license, in some cases by omission. It fails to inform the audience, for example, that Lawrence's repute is based not only on his legendary antics in the

Middle East but also, and equally, on his writings, which included *Seven Pillars of Wisdom* (privately published), a classic of warfare. Nonetheless, the film does provide insight into the very complex personality which fills a special niche in any study of leadership.

Indeed, a student of leadership qualities can learn a great deal from Lawrence of Arabia. In the field, among the tribes of what would become Arabia, he displayed many laudable leadership attributes. He was strategic, courageous, visionary, inspirational and even charismatic. But this perception of Lawrence was unique to the desert. In his traditional hidebound British homeland, he was perceived by most as reckless, dreamy, unfocused, impertinent, undisciplined and a loner. Here was a man who, taken out of his own environment, blossomed into a revered leader. He is an example to one and all of the potential in many of us to shine as leaders when provided with the surrounding or situation that brings out our hidden best.

Metamorphosis Under the Leadership Mantle

This leadership phenomenon is not to be confused with the performance of leaders like a Harry S. Truman, say, who rise up to meet the challenges of the times. President Truman is often used as an example of the office making the man and not the other way around. Nor is Thomas Lawrence an example of the many individuals who assume leadership by rising to the challenges offered in disastrous circumstances, like the ordinary man cum hero who is thrust into a leadership role of sorts when he helps to rescue injured passengers from a plane crash or pulls a victim from a burning car. Those are acts borne of circumstances that will most likely never be replicated or alter the life of the rescuer, although the psychological impacts of the rescue may be very real. The mystery and the power of Lawrence is that he became a different person under the mantle of leadership. The quality that enabled that change, and the one that will be examined in this chapter, is adaptability. No character in literature or in real life is a more compelling example of adaptability than Thomas Edward Lawrence.

The film generally, albeit romantically, tracks his life from his early army days as an unremarkable (save for his citations for insubordination) officer who is offered and accepts assignment to the Arabian Peninsula as a representative to King Feisel. This piece chronicles Lawrence's relationship with the King and the King's tribal leaders and his leadership of the King's armies against the Turks. The portrayal of the role of the American media in lionizing the exploits of Lawrence in the world press is accurate. *New York Times* reporter Jackson Bentley followed Lawrence during many of his adventures and captured them in words and photographs for the world to admire. In large part, the publicity generated as a result contributed to Lawrence's own belief that he was larger than life.

Several scenes are worthy of exploration for what they can instruct about leadership. The first begins when he arrives in the desert. As he embarks on his trek from Cairo, Lawrence is provided with a native guide and takes up the difficult task of camel riding while learning to survive in the desert environment that he would come to love. To many, this environment would have been daunting, but to Lawrence it was love at first sight. He took to its challenges with obvious delight and showed respect to his mentor, a likeable member of one of the many warring tribes of Arabia.

In the first demonstration of how adaptable Lawrence will prove to be, the duo comes to a halt atop their camels. As both men look out at the never-ending sameness of the blazing horizon, Lawrence begins to pour a cup of water from a leather pouch and offers it to his guide. The guide demurs with the proud pronouncement that he does not need the drink, because "I am a Bedouin," referring, of course, to the fact that he is a native of the country and has, therefore, himself adapted to the heat. Lawrence looks him in the eye and pours the water back into the pouch, announcing, "I will drink when you drink." It is in this scene that the cloth for Lawrence's style of leadership is cut. He is determined to understand the culture and the environment and to adopt them as his own. He is determined to adapt.

The Magic of Adaptability

Adaptability is defined by *The American Heritage Dictionary* as follows: "Capable of adapting or of being adapted." In defining adaptation, it goes on to say that it is "the act of changing to a new or special use or situation." Lawrence displayed an extraordinary ability to adapt to change. He could even be described as vicissitudinous, that is, characterized by his own changes or shifts in being in response to the world around him. I know of no one in fact or in fiction who had this protagonist's flair for adaptability; and it was this adaptability over a long period that was the very underpinning of his successful leadership of the tribal armies. It was an adaptability that went beyond merely adapting to the harsh physical environment, the heat and the barrenness of the desert. That would have been difficult enough in itself, but there are many examples of the hero's even greater facility for understanding the culture and mores of the tribes of the region and using that knowledge to further buttress his considerable leadership skills. This cultural adaptability was equally important to Lawrence's reputation.

Lawrence's cultural adaptability is illustrated throughout this picture of his life in the desert, but never more clearly than in the series of scenes concerning the tribal member who falls from his camel during a night march across a particularly hostile stretch of desert. As dawn looms, an empty camel saddle attests to his mishap. The leader of the tribe, informed of his subordinate's absence, also sees the soldier's riderless camel. With matter-of-fact casualness, the leader declares, "He will die...it is written." Lawrence is outraged and appalled and demands that the group return to find the man, but the tribal leader flatly denies the request. So, our hero starts out alone on what is seemingly a suicide mission, declaring as he goes that, "Nothing is written, except here," pointing to his head and galloping toward the now rising and deadly sun. The leader demands, but to no avail, that Lawrence return to finish the assault on the sea that he had started. After a time, when all hope for his return has diminished, the troops are thrilled by the sight of the bedraggled Lawrence, barely alive upon his camel with the rescued man clinging to him and the camel for life.

The natives view this act of courage almost as a miracle. Here Lawrence displays how, in a phrase we've all come to know so well, he "walks the talk"—proving he is willing, on the one hand, to adapt and, on the other, insisting on adhering to his own principles. The message is so powerful that the tribal members adopt him as one of their own, even donning him with the native dress of the desert. Lawrence has truly *become* one of them.

The final and most compelling example of Lawrence's adaptability comes after he uses his guile to persuade a rival tribal leader to join up with him and his competing tribe in attacking the Turkish-held town of Aqaba. Mistrust abounds as the two factions make camp on the night before the attack on the Turks. The scene fades in at dusk as this simple task is undertaken.

A shot rings out, and Lawrence runs to the center of the hubbub occurring at the scene of the shot. One man lies dead at the hands of a rival tribal member. Lawrence is told that it was the conclusion of an old family feud. The two tribes make preparations for retribution, which will beget more retribution and an eventual mini-civil war, a result that would be much to the favor of the Turks but to the considerable dismay of Lawrence. As the apparently inevitable confrontation commences, our hero grabs a pistol and takes command. He cries out to one of the leaders, "If the offender pays with his life, will you be satisfied?" The reply is in the affirmative. Lawrence turns to the other leader and inquires, "If they do not take revenge on your man, will you be satisfied?" Again, there comes an affirmative response. Our hero now must act.

With this agreement in hand, Lawrence marches off to confront the assassin, pronouncing "Then I will execute the man myself and everyone will be satisfied." It is only as Lawrence approaches the guards holding the killer on the ground that the man's identity becomes known to our hero. To everyone's surprise, he is the same man that Lawrence risked his life to save just days before. With anguish showing on every line of his face, but with little hesitation, Lawrence raises his weapon and fires into the man until the gun is empty and the man is dead.

Adaptability Based on Understanding

In this scene, Lawrence is the epitome of physical and cultural adaptability. He has come to understand the nature of the tribal customs and conflicts of the region. He has already begun to envision all of the tribes becoming one to form a unified Arabia. He also knows that he has to find a way to bridge the gap between the tribes to facilitate that unification. To move his vision toward reality, Lawrence overcomes his aversion to violence and his feelings for the man whose life he is about to take. Lawrence would not have been able to take this step if he had not adapted to the culture of the region, first by coming to understand it and then by designing behavior which commanded respect within that culture. It is probably not surprising that the tribes were in constant awe of T. E. Lawrence. They marveled at his courage and his ability to become one of them. Some of the tribal members almost deified him, and there was enough ham in our hero that he did not disabuse them of the thought that he was god-like. He often believed his own headlines.

At Lawrence's burial services, the *New York Times* reporter Bentley spoke of Lawrence as "a poet, a scholar, a mighty warrior and a shameless exhibitionist." As to the last, Lawrence never missed a photo-op, which is why there is a considerable library of his exploits in the archives of the photographs at the *New York Times*. Sophisticated in the ways of the media, Lawrence understood how it could help him achieve his vision.

On several occasions during his two year tenure in the Middle East, Lawrence returned to Cairo for additional resources and the reassurances of his superiors that England had no aspirations in Arabia save only to rid it of the Turks. He succeeded in his aims on those excursions but was each time ridiculed behind his back and used by the powers-that-be to gain support from the tribes from whom they would later hold back artillery and the other resources needed to make them truly independent. After each visit, Lawrence would be described as "going native," a derogatory characterization of Lawrence as someone who had adopted the local habits to such an extent as to make him indistinguishable from the indigenous population.

Each time he returned to Arabia, Lawrence left more of himself there as he shed more of his English skin. He was the English version of The Man of LaMancha, tilting at windmills.

Seen by some as a negative, it was really through Lawrence's ability to adopt local habits as his own, to adapt, that he was able to score a series of major successes. He rallied the rival tribes to capture the port at Aqaba. He gained the support of the British leadership in getting the necessary resources to outfit a modest indigenous army, which he exhorted to stunning victories over the Turks, who were, as a result, denied the use of the extensive railroad lines. Finally, Lawrence led the army of King Feisal in its defeat of the forces defending Damascus. And these were but a few of his successful exploits.

Simply creating a well-led army which kept the Turks occupied while the British attacked other cities was a major contribution to British success. No citizen of the crown ever more fully absorbed, or was more fully absorbed into, the Middle Eastern culture than T.E. Lawrence. Certainly, he was without peer in the significant consequences of that absorption.

Some of the lessons in leadership to be taken from Lawrence leap out at us. To be successful, a leader must, like Lawrence, be adaptable. Lawrence also was possessed of some of the other key qualities of leadership. He was driven by his vision of a unified people made up of the many tribes in Arabia; and, as a visionary alone, he is to be admired. In addition, Lawrence had a pronounced integrity, an adherence to his own principles, which never wavered in the face of controversy. There are still other qualities that should be observed, but not necessarily emulated, in our hero. His physical courage many times bordered on the reckless. His confidence in himself, in his strategy and his vision often crossed the line into arrogance. He so adapted to his environment that he sometimes became a caricature of himself.

Above all, Lawrence is an example of a leader whose leadership ability only reached maturity, perhaps only came into being, under very special circumstances. It is doubtful that, left in a traditional assignment in Cairo or London, Lawrence would have evolved as a candidate for a major motion picture or mention with the likes of Lord Nelson. The extreme circumstances in which he found himself brought out the best in Lawrence. In a far-off land with no one to judge or control him, he acquired the freedom to allow his intellect and principles to mold his actions. There, out of sight or sound of his homeland, he was perceived as a leader, and, as someone who evolved into what people perceived him to be, he became a clear example of someone who rises to the occasion.

Leaders Ask "Why Not?"

The real lesson for those who are seeking to hone their leadership skills may be that what you see is not necessarily what you get. When you observe or judge the leadership potential of others, you need to allow for the possibility that some individuals can exceed even their own perceptions of their talents. Likewise, when you are serving as a leader and are faced with a seemingly insurmountable challenge, delve deeper into the challenge and yourself and search out the inner strength that may be hidden just below the surface. In doing so, learn to question the status quo or the "we tried that before and it didn't work" attitude. Try to adopt the approach once attributed to Robert Kennedy by his brother Ted during Robert's eulogy, "Some men see things as they are and say why. I dream things that never were and say, why not." It is this kind of mentality that was instrumental in driving Lawrence to save the young man in the desert, a mentality that is embodied in Lawrence's declaration as he points to his head: "Nothing is written except here." He was saying that if you can envision it, you can make it so, without the constraints that may come from other people and old ways of thinking.

A Deafening Drumbeat

Lawrence marched to the beat of his own drummer. Because this was his approach, he was able to believe to the depths of his soul what most of the rest of the world found to be impossible—that there would one day be a united Saudi Arabia. Lawrence believed he could do things that had never been done, because he was able to envision them and to rely on the legitimacy of those visions. He could ride a camel across an uncrossed desert, he could lead an unleadable rabble. And because he followed his own visions, he could be perceived as a heroic savior on one continent while being seen as a bumbling fool on another.

Lawrence was no fool. Admittedly, he acted the fool on occasion, but he was always the British gentleman. He was also a scholar, writing several important books on war as well as some wonderful poems of literary note. He was also a wit of some renown. At a cocktail party in Egypt on a day of intense heat, Lawrence was approached by a lady of uncertain age who had a reputation for trying to get close to famous people. Using the heat wave as a conversational opening, she remarked, "Ninety-two today, Colonel Lawrence. Just think of it, ninety-two!" Lawrence eyed her coolly and replied dryly, "Many happy returns, Madam." Lawrence was erudite and educated. His richly-layered character is clearly suitable for close study by students of leadership.

The abiding tenacity exuded by Lawrence is to be particularly admired and emulated. You can take his positive traits, not the least of which is his adaptability, and practice them in almost every project with improved success being the possible result. Adapt to the culture of the customer. Adapt to the changing employee culture. Adapt to the vagaries of the economy. Adapt to the ebb and flow of the political environment, that of the company and that of the country. Adapt to the various and inevitable challenges of every project or program, and that adaptability will serve you well as a leader.

THE CONTENDER
Integrity

"Strange Bedfellows"

We live in a world with a cacophony of real-time news. The reporting of what is happening, when it is happening is an industry larger than any multi-national industrial giant. So-called 24/7 news is as commonplace as "Made in China" labels. We are saturated with news that is not only reported but analyzed, reanalyzed and replayed. News and what is being said about it has given rise to Russert and Rush and King, and Rather and Cronkite before them. CNN has had to make way for ESPN, SKY NEWS, ESPN 2, CNN HEADLINE NEWS, MSNBC and a host of other news outlets of one sort or another. With the internet, the sources of news and what passes as news have grown exponentially.

But while weather and crime take up much of the airwaves, they are bested by politics in the contest for exposure. It seems that we cannot escape. The Electoral College had only just cast its ballots formalizing the reelection of President Bush—and the Supreme Court had not even spoken—when the analysis of who would run for the office in 2008 provided the fodder for the latest political prognostication. Politics provide anyone who wishes to study leadership traits and qualities a panoply of material replete with examples of those traits and qualities.

We watch politicians on a daily basis, and we see a stunning array of characteristics and qualities—courage, stupidity, wisdom, candor, obfuscation and directness, to name a few. It can go from the ridiculous to the sublime, and it is easy to see why politics and politicians have lent themselves to scores of cinematic renditions. We have, for example, "Mr. Deeds" of going to Washington fame, a fictional icon; the equally captivating *All The President's Men* capitalized on our real-life fascination with the travails of the Nixon Administration.

Everyday news-watching gave us the charismatic Clinton and the shaking of the finger during the "I did not have..." speech that blew us all away. But probably the best movie look at politics played out against the backdrop of multimedia culture is *The Contender*. While it was not a box office blockbuster, with all of its plots and subplots and side stories, *The Contender* offers gripping interest. It also provides some excellent examples of many positive leadership traits and qualities and some traits that do not serve leaders well.

The film is set in the present and covers only about a month in real time. It is the story of the attempt by the President of the United States to fill the office of Vice-President, left vacant by the death of the incumbent. The dominant character in the film is the President himself, but our protagonist is his designee to fill the vacancy. Laine Billings Hanson is the Senator from Ohio, and she must go through the usual hoops to be confirmed by the chairman of the cognizant committee who is a member of the opposing party. At the same time, Senator Hanson is undergoing the mandated scrutiny from several investigative agencies like the FBI. Meanwhile, the media and the newly energized internet bloggers are providing non-stop coverage on every aspect of the process, to say nothing of every one of Senator Hanson's peccadillos that can be dredged up.

Prior to the first public hearing, allegations surface that the Senator was involved in a wild sexcapade while a freshman in college. The allegations are accompanied by photographs which appear to depict her performance of sex acts to the cheers of several onlookers. The files which contain the photos have supposedly been purloined from the office of the villain of the piece, Congressman Sheldon Runyon, and a member of his staff leaks a copy of the photos to Senator Hanson's assistant.

Congressman Runyon is a right-wing zealot who has a negative history with the President, Jackson Evans, and who has made it clear that his support for the vice-presidential replacement goes to Governor Hathaway who has received praise for some recent heroics. These heroics receive a goodly portion of the film's attention in the opening scenes. (In addition to these major players, there are a number of minor players who are also worth observing for the leadership lessons they reveal as the drama unfolds.)

Resolute, Test After Test

The heroine in this cinematic political treatise was chosen by the President because she clearly and consistently displayed integrity, a prerequisite for good leadership. The fact that she is a *woman* with this quality is not lost on the advisors to the President. For men and women alike, integrity is universally identified in courses, conferences and books as being among the three most important qualities for successful leaders. There are many synonyms for this quality, including honesty, uprightness, honor, truthfulness and character, and Senator Hanson seems to have them all. In test after test, she remains resolute, as we witness in more than one scene.

In the first such scene, just before having to appear before the Congressman's committee and the public, the Senator meets with the President's chief of staff to view the shocking photos that are about to be shown to the world. She is disgusted by the scenes which are depicted. She is brutally confronted by Chief of Staff Newman who excoriates her for the dilemma that the allegations have created for the President and asks her to "do the right thing." The right thing is, of course, understood to be voluntarily withdrawing her name from consideration.

The idea that she should withdraw her nomination is resisted by the Senator, who expresses the view that the President would not want her to cut and run because of these allegations, which are, after all, purely personal. The Senator remains poised but is clearly troubled when the Chief of Staff goes on to suggest, "Well then, just deny it...just deny it." This is the first test of her integrity that we observe. The set is the President's outer office, and she never cowers, never slouches and never relinquishes her poise. She remains cool and confident in her reply to the invitation to deny it. "It is below my dignity, and I will not." The frustrated Chief of Staff, clearly looking for the expedient way out, looks to an aide and asks if they can dig up some dirt on the self-righteous Congressman. With her integrity thus tested for a second time, the Senator stops him to offer her opinion that, "We would be no better than him if we did that." Through all of this, the quality of Senator Hanson's character, what she is all about, is eminently clear. She is prepared to do battle, but she will do it honorably and on her own terms.

Leaders are often confronted with situations that, while differing in their particulars, have the same effect: they put the leader's integrity to the test. And many leaders have failed in this regard, sometimes very publicly. Some have even risked going to prison, by misstating the numbers on the financial reports or other illegal actions. Some of these misdeeds clearly stem from greed, while some may have come from a misguided belief that it is for some good, for example to benefit the stockholders. The result, however, is the same in all cases. There is a moral breach, a failure of integrity. On a smaller scale, failures of integrity occur every day, by employees who exaggerate their resumes, for example, or employees who fail to own up to mistakes, adopting in both cases an "end justifies the means" or a "What harm will it do?" approach. They tell the truth but not the whole truth. You all know them, the ones who push the envelope and opt for the short cuts. Our protagonist here is of a different sort and demonstrates a depth of real integrity as she continues to be tested and always passes.

In the first scene, where she meets privately with and is confronted directly by the Congressional Chairman, he ridicules her and promises her no mercy if she does not wilt. He makes it clear that he will brutalize her in public. He unveils himself as the misanthrope that he is. Still, she refuses to take the easy way out and, instead, boldly stands her ground.

In the next scene, we find the Senator at her first public committee hearing. Of course, all of the trappings of a congressional hearing are enhanced for the movie audience as the drama builds. During this and other hearing scenes, the committee members maintain a veneer of courtesy, while pursuing questions that have the thinly-disguised purpose of discrediting the nominee for the vice-presidential office.

At one point, Congressman Runyon suggests he should pursue legislation to stop internet intrusion into personal lives. He then takes the opportunity to announce the address of the web site that has just posted the pictures of the orgy that purport-edly includes the Senator. Feigning shock at the allegations, the Chairman asks, "Senator, would you like to take this opportunity to deny these scurrilous charges?" The movie audience is repulsed by the Chairman's transparent antics but gets the sense that he is winning the battle of wits. The Senator is visibly shaken, as much by the description of the allegations as by the underhandedness of the Congressman, but she calmly replies, "I will have no response." She goes on to stake her ground by announcing, "I won't address the issue of sexuality, and I will not dignify these allegations with a response." Sensing an edge, the Chairman and his cronies on the committee go on to attack Hanson's positions, first her views on religion and then her decision to take maternity leave when she had a child. The enemy senses a rout of sorts and presses the per-ceived advantage.

In between hearings, several subplots are unfolding in the film; all manner of muck begins to be raked. The suggestion is made that the Senator may have received payment for the college sex act in which she is alleged to have engaged, thereby inferring that she may have committed prostitution. It is also revealed that she had a sexual relationship with her best friend's husband, who subsequently became the Senator's husband. Of course, this rev-elation opens her to further ridicule.

Resisting Victory

Just when all seems to be lost, a life buoy is thrown to our heroine, and the tide appears to be turning. The Senator is handed undeniable and irrefutable proof that the Chairman's wife had an abortion without his knowledge. As the publication of this report would cripple his very public and vehement anti-abortion position, it is just the ammunition to retaliate and strike the Chairman a lethal blow. This is in the heat of the hearings, as the Congressman continues to press his advantage to the point that provides Senator Hanson an opportunity to deliver her coup de grace. She is visibly torn as she considers the decision she is faced with, but in the end she chooses not to unleash the ultimate weapon. This is in keeping with her tenet of not getting down in the mud with the animals. She backs off, even at the risk of great personal humiliation. The time has come for a sit-down with the President.

The ever-present Chief of Staff Newman is present again when the Senator and the President have their meeting. Mr. Newman begs Laine to, "Give us something, and fight back!" She sits stoically and says that she is fully prepared to step down, but she will not respond to the charges. The President addresses her for the first time, saying "Fight back. Confess." She looks startled, but he continues, "Just confess, and tell everyone how there are lessons to be learned about underage drinking and youthful sex. Just confess. It will defuse the entire matter." Kermit Newman enthusiastically agrees, "That's it, just confess." She steels herself, and her countenance is deliberate when she replies with finality, "I understand how you feel Kermit, but it's just none of their business." Turning to the President, the Senator says that she will do whatever he directs her to do. The integrity she has so unflinchingly shown seems to be contagious when the President tells her, "In your closing statement, you go out there and show them why I chose you Laine."

It is hard to contemplate being in such a position. Imagine, if you will, being in a similar situation with the chief executive officer of a corporation or other organization, and give some thought to whether you could maintain your composure and, better still, whether you could stick to your principle. Could you withstand the pressure from the executives who literally have your future in their hands? Would you feel secure enough in your convictions, confident that you would be content with not having betrayed yourself, whatever the result? Does this even define integrity? Whether or not it's part of your own definition, there's something to be said about having the courage of your convictions, and in this film you can see the test of that characteristic contextually by watching the story unfold.

Beware the Hidden Advantage

Before you decide what you would do, there is one more part of the story that you should take into account. Prior to Senator Hanson's meeting with the President, she was given a secret affidavit that could serve as irrefutable evidence that she was innocent of all of the allegations. Does it change your thoughts about how you might act in the Senator's shoes if you knew that you had the winning hand? Imagine that you can see everyone's hole card, and you know that you can't be beaten. As a leader, it is the times when you have the hidden advantage that your behavior will best reflect your character and reveal whether or not you have integrity.

As the underdog or the underling, it's not hard to act humble because, in fact, you are humble. But a better test of your character is how you behave, how you carry yourself, when you are the prohibitive favorite. How then do you react? The test of integrity is how you act in victory, not in defeat. It's a lesson this film drives home in an unambiguous way that should commend it to aspiring leaders.

The penultimate scene in the film crystallizes the message. The President, portrayed as a practical politician who at times engages in situational ethics, had set a trap for Congressman Runyon and insured the positive vote for his designee. The scene is set on the grounds of the White House at nighttime and finds the President and the Senator savoring the comeuppance for the Chairman when the trap was sprung. Both seem to express that it couldn't have happened to a more deserving fellow. They are feeling good and enjoying some fine wine as they settle on the expansive plush lawn.

The President is in a playful mood and says, "I am dying to know what happened on that night at the party. Off the record and just between Jackson and Laine, what happened?" She smiles and repeats, "Just between us?" When the President nods, she begins a description of the events in question.

Truth Is a Good Thing

She tells him that she had, in fact, gotten drunk and agreed to go to a side room with two of the frat brothers. She says there was no truth to the allegation of her being disrobed, but she did go into the bedroom with them. She goes on to explain that one of the boys exposed himself to her. When she hesitates, the President smiles and encourages her to continue. She says that she took one of the young men's members in her hand and looked at him. She giggles as she goes on to say that she looked at it and said, "I'm sorry, I don't smoke." With that, both she and the President laughed. "That was it?" he said smiling. "Yep, and then I got the hell out of there." A bemused look falls over the President, "What about the pictures? What about the eye witnesses?" That wasn't me. I have a large birthmark which is not shared by the girl in the photos. The witnesses were simply the stuff of urban legend." He is shocked. "Why on earth did you not tell your president?" Exasperated, she responds, "Because, sir, it was none of your business."

The President recovers after a moment of speechlessness. He knowingly tells her that the exculpatory evidence that has been brought forth is dynamite. She nods and smiles her agreement. He announces his strategy, "Tomorrow, we will have a press conference, I will unveil the new evidence, and your nomination will sail through within hours." His facial expressions show his pride at the victory, but she cools his mood with her response. "No, sir, no press conference." She is determined to let the process take its course. "But you have won," the President protests, "you can tell the world the truth." Her expression tells him what she is thinking. She looks at him and, without words, her entire being shouts, "You still don't get it".

There is a long pause, as Senator Hanson is preparing to tell the President of the United States what the events leading up to this moment have been about. In fact, the good Senator is going to reveal to the audience the film's message, when she says, "Sir, principles only mean something if you stick with them when they are inconvenient." She might have added that principles are especially important only when you have all of the facts, but it is principles that can provide the strength to withstand adversity.

This is not a subtle piece that calls upon our intellect to decipher some hidden meaning but a film whose message is obvious and whose meaning is unequivocal. The point of the story is reflected in the heroine, as the movie delivers its message forcefully. At the same time, like the Senator herself, the film is professional in its style and delivery, offering an excellent vehicle for a study in integrity and principles.

While many of the main leadership lessons to be found in *The Contender* are self-evident, the film abounds with a number of ancillary lessons that are worthy of consideration as well. The character of the Congressman from Delaware, for example, certainly provides some food for leadership thought, as do the spouses of the major players. Again, these lessons, like the lesson at the heart of the story, are not subtle; but, though easy to discern, they are worth your viewing time and what you can make of them.

It is integrity, though, that predominates in this cinematic look at the world of politics. Senator Laine Hanson is confronted in almost every scene with challenges to her principles. She is pressured to compromise, not just by other people but also by the desire to achieve, the desire to be accepted, the desire to please superiors, the desire to be admired and the desire to be valued. With all of this pressing in favor of bending her principles, the Senator at no time is hesitant, at no time does she waver, and at no time does she compromise. In this regard, she is a character we can all strive to imitate.

With all its directness, there is a certain cleverness in the way the film's message is delivered. We come to be on the Senator's side not because we admire her stance on principle but because we admire her grit and determination. Our gut reaction is that we want to see her fight back. We hope that she will use the secret weapon to annihilate her antagonist. We want her to win because she is not as bad as the rest of the players, not because she is inherently good. Still, at the end of the day, most viewers will conclude that we would be fortunate to have a Vice-President like Laine Billings Hanson and that we would do well to emulate her integrity.

APOLLO 13
Innovation

"Moonstruck"

In his speech to the Congress of the United States on May 25, 1961, John Fitzgerald Kennedy, the poster-child for charisma, articulated a vision and offered a challenge when he said, "I believe this nation should commit itself to achieving the goal, before this decade is out, of landing a man on the moon and returning him safely to earth." Thus began one of the most technologically complex endeavors man would undertake. While Tom Wolfe's *The Right Stuff* catalogs the selection and training of the original seven astronauts, it is *Apollo 13* that depicts in detail the many complexities of this incredible moon-landing mission.

There is an aspect of the nuclear power business and other industries known as "conduct of operations." It is, in essence, the unalterable and fastidious adherence to a highly structured set of principles and procedures that are exact, absolute and formally written. You are no doubt familiar with some aspects of conduct of operations practices, for example, the check-list followed by pilots before a flight to be certain beyond any doubt that everything has been attended to or the repeating of a ship captain's orders to ensure that they have been correctly heard and understood. The captain barks a command, "Right full rudder," and the sailor who will execute the command repeats, "Aye, aye, sir, right full rudder."

Many military and hazardous-environment workers are trained and drilled, often by rote, in these kinds of steps which are meant to guarantee the safety of the men and the mission. It is a "by the book" mentality, and there is little, if any, room for innovation or creativity in a conduct of operations environment. There is certainly no place for an "off the cuff" or "by the seat of your pants" action. The basis of the philosophy is that the most minute details of the seemingly simplest tasks, from the specific amount of torque to be applied to a bolt to the required grasping of handrails when taking the staircase, are not suggestions or guidelines but strict commandments that, if not adhered to, result in a reprimand or worse. The intent is that dangerous environments are reserved for "in the box" thinking and not for creativity, which can result in a mistake or an accident. Indeed, creativity is anathema to a conduct of operations environment.

Nowhere is the conduct of operations regimen more pronounced than in the United States space program. Mankind was riveted to every media form on July 20, 1969, when Neil Armstrong took that giant leap for all of us, and although we might not have thought of it as such, it was the high-water mark for conduct of operations. Yet, just two years earlier, we were sensitized to the dangers faced by space explorers as crew members Grissom, White and Chaffee perished in a blaze while being helplessly strapped into the burning hulk of Apollo 1. Funding for the space program was cut as there was a frantic search for the causes of the tragedy. We eventually learned about the combustibility of pure oxygen, about the thousands of miles of wiring and the sparks that led to the disaster.

So, NASA changed the makeup of the spacecraft's breathable air, aptly applying the lessons it learned and assuring that the enhanced conduct of operations—quite literally creating a zero-defect program—would yield success. What better evidence could there be than a successful moon mission? Following the success of Apollo 12, Apollo 13 looked almost routine.

In fact, however, this mission was destined to become the one on which the failproof systems failed, and massive creativity and innovation were required to prevent a tragedy. It is creativity and innovation that are explored in this chapter, with a particular focus on the role that creativity can play in even the most rigorous of structured environments.

Leadership and Creativity, Both Difficult to Define

Creativity is almost as difficult to define as leadership. *The American Heritage Dictionary* defines it as: "Having the ability or power to create" or "Characterized by originality and expressiveness; imaginative." What it means to innovate is no clearer: "To begin or introduce something new; be creative." A quote attributed to Edward M. Forster perhaps comes closest, advising that "In the creative state a man is taken out of himself. He lets down a bucket into his subconscious and draws up something which is normally beyond his reach. He mixes this thing with his normal experiences, and out of the mixture he makes a work of art." Leaders recognize this ability for what it is. Henry Ford, when told by an efficiency expert that one of his lead engineers appeared to be unproductive and constantly had his feet propped up on his desk, was said to have replied, "That man once had an idea that saved us millions of dollars and at that time I believe he had his feet planted where they are now."

Other leaders of industry and the world also demonstrate their understanding of the value and impact of creativity. Ross Perot once tried to deliver a Christmas package to every U.S. serviceman held captive by the North Vietnamese. He was denied permission to deliver them directly with his fleet of 727's and informed that policy dictated that no U.S. commercial plane would receive permission. He flew the packages to Moscow, used the Russian postal system to mail the packages to the prisons, and they reached their destination. Perot was not to be denied by established policies or procedures. Apollo 13 would face unprecedented and monumental challenges that would, likewise, demand something more than what could be discerned from established policies and procedures.

Film director Ron Howard drew upon the real-life drama to put together a rousing film rendition of the times. (You may remember director Howard from his role as Richie on *Happy Days*.) The *Apollo 13* docudrama makes full use of the state-of-the-art sound systems to blast the space capsule into space, and the viewers feel they are along for the ride. The presentation is replete with patriotic innuendo, bordering on jingoism. The astronauts are all-American males, complete with crew cuts and adoring women, wives and mothers prepared to make whatever sacrifices might be required to support their men.

Star-Crossed

The story revolves around the eventual crew of Apollo 13, and Commander James Lovell is the hero at its center. As we briefly meet Lovell's family and extended family, made up of his brother astronauts and their families, Howard provides glimpses of the 70's culture with scenes of Corvettes and bouffant hairdos. There is no mention of the brutal war in Viet Nam or the controversy swirling around the Nixon White House. This is a feel-good movie about real live American heroes and role models. In more ways than one, this motion picture is mission-oriented.

Apollo 13 seemed almost star-crossed from the outset. In keeping with the superstitions surrounding the mission's numerical order in the space program, the original and secondary crew members selected were beset with odd maladies. Allen Shepard, the first American in space, was scheduled to command Apollo 13, only to be besieged by an ear infection that required him to surrender his seat to another veteran astronaut, Jim Lovell. Lovell, with as much time in space as any of his comrades, seemed a good choice, and preparations for the flight into space continued. Then, just three days before the scheduled launch, it was learned that astronaut Ken Mattingly might have been exposed to measles, so Mattingly was replaced by Jack Swigert. In the scene, Mattingly is visibly agitated when Lovell breaks the news that he is being replaced, and Lovell appropriately accepts accountability for the decision. Lovell could have laid the decision to replace Mattingly at the Flight Director's doorstep; instead, he looked Mattingly in the eye and said, "This was my call Ken." The Commander was in command.

The crew changes were a portent of a troubled flight. The great understatement of all time, "Houston we have a problem," was uttered by pilot Jack Swigert and then repeated by Commander Lovell at a time when even they had not yet grasped the magnitude of the system failure they were facing. An explosion from a ruptured oxygen tank in the service module had caused a myriad of puzzling problems. Among other things, the fuel cells supplying power to the spacecraft faltered, the pressure in the oxygen tanks began to decline threateningly, and the craft began changing its attitude (orientation in space).

The unimaginable became reality, and the hordes of experts in the control room were confronted with a bewildering barrage of calamities. There was a quadruple failure, a pair of double failures within systems designed with redundant controls. Even the simulator, designed to create almost unthinkable situations and allow the astronauts to train to respond to them, never anticipated the challenges that would face this entire team. These disastrous failures occurred just three days into the mission and set the stage for a level of unprecedented creativity and innovation.

The astronauts' lives were now, as never before, in the hands of mission control. Mission control was under the leadership of veteran Gene Kranz, and it was Kranz who now took command. After getting systems updates from each of multiple section leaders, Kranz admonished the team, saying, "Let's work the problem people, let's not make the problem worse by guessing." Each of the NASA-manned spacecraft was profoundly complex, and repairing one during a mission, on the fly as it were, required a detailed and intricate analysis of all of the interacting components. Mission plans and procedures, developed over many months, had to be reworked and rewritten under severe time constraints. This was anything but simple, but the Kranz approach to the job that had to be done was simple: "Failure is not an option." Save for his chain-smoking, he was the epitome of self-control and confidence.

When the catastrophe occurred, mission control was a sea of engineers glued to their computer screens, which were backlit with charts and graphs on every conceivable system, valve and filter. As they looked for a solution, each human cluster was in a high degree of anxiety, searching for anomalies that could have caused the problem. All the while, film cameras were catching it for posterity.

Kranz was surrounded by some of the greatest technical minds in the world and recognized his responsibility to effectively motivate them to abandon the strict conduct of operations mentality that they lived by and to extol them to embrace innovativeness. All communications to the astronauts continued to be delivered with yoga-like calmness, belying the frenetic activity on the crippled spacecraft and in the control room. Now firmly in command, Kranz ordered all support teams to be alerted and activated. He called for constant status reports and, amidst a sea of chaos, Kranz remained an island of tranquility.

Trust Equals Confidence

One of the key technicians arrived at a conclusion that the astronauts had to shut down two of the three fuel cells to stop a leak. He concluded that, if left unattended, the leak would most certainly doom the Apollo 13 crew to suffocation. This conclusion to shut down the fuel cells was not obvious to any of the other team members, and following this advice would insure failure of the mission to land on the moon. All eyes were on the engineer as he made his case to Kranz; everyone recognized the dire implication for the mission. With yet another display of leadership, this time in the form of trust in his team, Kranz gave the order to shut down the fuel cells. When Lovell received the order, the impact of compliance was not lost on him. Instead of immediately instituting the order, Lovell uncharacteristically questioned his leader asking, "Are you sure, Houston?" "That's affirmative," came the response. Commander Lovell complied, but not before saying for crew and mission control members to hear, "We've lost the moon."

Trust in subordinates, fundamental to good leaders, reflects a leader's confidence. Good leaders are confident in the people they have selected (or inherited) and confident in the plan they have devised or adopted. Leaders have to depend on assessment and foresight, not on hindsight and second-guessing. As is always the case, one leadership quality, here creativity, may be central to successfully navigating the course in a given situation. But there will be other qualities, like the trust shown in the scene described, that come into play in a significant way. There is still more to learn.

The systems failure on Apollo 13 exacerbated an already delicate situation. For example, having shut down two of the three fuel cells, the astronauts were forced to abandon the command module to conserve energy. They repaired to the LEM (the lunar excursion module), which forced them to execute several remaining tactical commands from a unit ill-designed for the tasks confronting them. Eventually, even the LEM had to have its power turned off to conserve enough energy to ensure reentry. Without power in the LEM, the astronauts suffered frigid temperatures, that, along with lack of sleep, stagnant air and severe rationing of water, were taking their toll on the morale and physical well-being of these heroes. Hayes was running a 104-degree fever as conditions deteriorated. Worse yet, the rapid creation of carbon dioxide threatened to overtake them unless they could filter the air. Kranz and his team were now faced with an imminent threat—the astronauts would die without filtered air.

Be Creative... Now!

When informed of the new challenge, Kranz calmly suggested that the filters from the command module be used. Unfortunately, he was advised by his team at mission control that the command module had square filters and the LEM was fitted with round ones. Without skipping a beat, Kranz commanded the team to figure out a way to "fit a square peg into a round hole, and do it quick." The next scene opens with half a dozen engineers around a conference table. One of the harried men empties a large box on the table, and holding up a shoebox-sized item and a tube resembling a half-gallon soft drink container, he announces that they are charged with "fitting one of these into one of these, using this stuff." With that pronouncement, he dumped onto the table a bizarre assortment of hoses, filters, tape, cardboard containers and other items that the astronauts had on the craft. The magnitude of the task is not lost on the team...or the viewing audience.

In the meantime, the misfortunes on the crippled spacecraft did not abate. The LEM, which was intended to house two men on the surface of the moon for a short period and then return to the fully stocked command module, was now a lifeboat for three men and required them to perform maneuvers that it was not specifically designed to do with reduced power and questionable mechanical capabilities. Teams on the ground, continuously challenged by Kranz to come up with solutions, were frantically working to head off disaster. When Kranz asks a representative of the LEM's manufacturer how the craft might respond to meet the expected difficulties, the representative responds defensively, "We designed the LEM to land on the moon and return to the command module." At this cop-out, Kranz shows his exasperation by raising his voice to just below a shout and responding, "I'm not interested in what it was designed to do, I'm interested it what it can do!"

Watching this exchange, you cannot help but conclude that Kranz's words and tone are in earnest but are also formulated to have the effect of demanding more than stock answers and by-the-book thinking. The encounter was not lost on the team members who bore witness. Kranz was issuing a challenge to one and all to use creativity as the new measure of potential solutions.

After a time, the team working the CO_2 crisis bursts into the mission control amphitheater with a strange looking contraption, and the team leader announces, "This is what they have to make." "This" was an odd configuration made up of duct tape, plastic bags, Velcro® and tubes of various materials. The key communicator to the astronauts, Jack Lousma, inquired as to whether or not the team had drafted procedures for the stranded flight crew to follow to assemble the device. With a look of satisfaction, the lead engineer turns over a sheaf of crumbled papers, and Lousma communicates to the crew that he has a fix for the CO_2 problem and he will walk them through the procedures.

The crew, now hobbled by lack of fresh filtered air, was able to meet the challenge of fixing the filter supply and succeeded not a moment too soon. Still, other problems persisted, and Kranz had to continue to juggle all the balls of adversity that were airborne.

Among the potentially life-threatening circumstances that remained, the severely curtailed power supply continued to be problematic with regard to the requirements for reentry. As a precaution, all of the systems, including the computer systems, had been shut down to conserve energy and had to be restarted. The electrical load requirements for the restart were being calculated by yet another expert team that was taking every potential sequencing process and testing and retesting it in the simulator.

Each time a new sequence was simulated, it drew more than the maximum four amps, which the sequence had to stay below for the systems restart to succeed. Ken Mattingly, who as it turned out did not succumb to measles after all, was rushed to the simulator to attempt the infinite permutations of sequencing and

VELCRO® is a registered trademark of VELCRO Industries, B.V.

to race against the clock for a solution. Meanwhile, the wounded spacecraft was plummeting toward the fiery reentry point.

Kranz made the decision to direct the crew to effect an engine burn, allowing for the correct entry angle, without the aid of the computers in order to facilitate the still problematic restart of the reentry systems. The mutual confidence and trust displayed by Kranz and the crew is manifest when the crew manually executes the directive, using the earth as a visual data point. Kranz displayed no hesitation as the command was flawlessly executed in accordance with the procedure. Now only the restart and the necessary power for reentry and splashdown remained between the team and success.

Thinking Outside the Simulator

In countless attempts to seek a sequence that would not exceed the punishingly low four amps, Ken Mattingly was the hands-on leader of the effort to develop a restart procedure. His frustration was growing as alarms went off time and again to signal that the limit was being exceeded. Finally, he had a new creative thought, a vision that went beyond the simulator. He recognized that he actually had *two* sources of power: what was in the LEM and whatever residual power was left in the command module itself. It was then that everyone agreed that the solution was to combine the two available power sources to meet the requisite limit.

By now, the anxious astronauts were questioning the knowledge of the ground crew, and Mattingly had to revert to a conduct of operations mentality approach to calm them and restore their confidence. Lovell takes comfort in the approach and appears visually relieved when he hears the soothing voice of his erstwhile crewmate, who assures the three on board Apollo 13 that he will walk them through the freshly-minted procedures to fire up the computer and the other power systems and bring them home. He did so in the comfortable envelope of conduct of operations.

The film's conclusion has the obligatory dramatic radio silence during reentry, as the audience views the families, the public in Times Square, the group at mission control, where the tension is palpable, and the stoic astronauts. Even though the outcome is a foregone conclusion, tears still well up as elation sweeps through every venue.

This motion picture is masterful in depicting the drama in mission control and on the spacecraft. The makers of the film are able to maintain an atmosphere of heightened suspense, even though virtually every viewer knows the outcome as a matter of historical fact. The scenes aboard the craft are able to very effectively capture the tension among the crew, which is played out alongside the relative chaos in mission control. Through it all, the astronauts and ground control never falter as they work their way through one extraordinary situation after another. They exchange factual data and affirm commands and understandings in cool, calm, almost automated voices, all very much in keeping with the conduct of operations approach in which they were so well schooled.

When Gene Kranz says "Let's work the problem people," it is implicit that the team must concentrate on identifying the problems and creating solutions. Kranz was not interested in excuses or pessimism or basic negativism, even questioning on occasion whether potential negative scenarios really needed to be conveyed to the crew or should be withheld because the information would serve no purpose. Failure was not an option as Kranz drove the team to creative solutions. Every decision he made was based on information that had a counter, and he had to choose between the two. More than anyone, he was responsible for the successful return of the crew.

There is a great connection between the order of mathematics and music. While we think of one as being part of the sciences and the other as being part of the arts, there is a precision associated with each. Indeed, there are few things more precise than a symphony. Yet even within the exactness of a composition, there is ample room for creativity of expression.

The Baton of Leadership

You can think of Gene Kranz as the orchestra leader and the crew as the three tenors. The rest of the players were the musicians, each sub-team a section of the orchestra. Kranz, holding the baton, was responsible to draw out the best from each section and each principal player, eliciting the tone and nuance that would create a successful performance. Like an orchestra leader, he was given the players and the musical score; like the maestro of leadership that he was, he took command and brought out the best in the team by putting his personal stamp on the performance.

Kranz succeeded in what can be a somewhat stifling conduct of operations environment. He himself was a fervent devotee of the conduct of operations discipline, and he could have been held hostage by the philosophy. Or he could, as he was able to do, allow that very discipline to help him focus on the innovation needed to get the required solutions and to implement them effectively. His ability to be creative and get others to do the same in an environment where creativity is not, as a rule, valued is striking. In his ability to adjust, in using creativity alongside rigor, Gene Kranz was the unsung leader of Apollo 13. The qualities that make him a superior leader are well worth observing by students of the craft.

ONE FLEW OVER THE CUCKOO'S NEST
Focus

"Even Paranoids Have Real Enemies"

He is R.P. McMurphy, the protagonist in the critically acclaimed film adaptation of the novel, *One Flew Over the Cuckoo's Nest*. His world may not be normal, but within that world he is, nevertheless, unquestionably a leader. The world of R.P. McMurphy is a state institution for the emotionally challenged. In the 50's, this facility might have been referred to as an insane asylum or the less politically sensitive "funny farm," and Mr. McMurphy is not the director or a staff member but is one of the residents.

This film is set early in the second half of the twentieth century. It opens with several sketches concerning the behavior of McMurphy. These snapshots in time depict a series of incidents which have, in sum, resulted in his institutional incarceration. The bulk of the picture is set within the confines of the hospital facility which is similar, one imagines, to all institutions of its type and in that era in America.

The characters that support the lead in the film are various and sundry other patients, each of whom has varying degrees of one mental disorder or other. These maladies range from anti-social behavior, as personified in R.P., to schizophrenia and catatonia, augmented by various physical abnormalities. As the film develops, it becomes apparent that McMurphy is what could be described as a very high-functioning mental defective who often displays many of the signs of normalcy. He is looked upon by some of his fellow inmates as a leader. Some of the patients look to him for direction and, indeed, they see him as a role model.

The villain of the piece is the psychiatric nurse who is in charge of the unit and the welfare of its inhabitants. Nurse Ratched is seen as a cruel, manipulative, controlling bureaucrat who may be herself half-crazed by the power she wields. The overarching theme of the film is the struggle between Ratched and McMurphy, and the supporting cast is caught up in the struggle. The inmates—and even the staff—bear the brunt of the fallout from the conflict.

While you may wonder at the selection of R.P. McMurphy as a role model for leadership qualities, the purpose of including him is to explore the specific quality that his character so vividly depicts. Leaders often emerge from the ranks and may assume leadership for many reasons. In most social and business structures, there is someone who is designated to be the leader, but the official leader may fail to lead or may relinquish the reins of control. Occasionally, in that case, control may be usurped by someone else. From a formal perspective, it is nurse Ratched who has been granted the mantle of leadership by virtue of her title and position, and it is R.P. who represents the classic subordinate. This juxtaposition of roles, and the reversal of roles that emerges, offers up a lesson that should be heeded.

Leading up to a pivotal scene that will be explored in detail in this chapter, the tensions between McMurphy and Ratched continue to build. His style of dealing with his environment is to challenge authority at every turn. Her inclination is to counter by using her position and authority to bow and bend him in the presence of the other patients and unit orderlies. It is a battle for the hearts and minds of the characters that have been cast in what becomes a play within the play.

The scene unfolds in the large dayroom which is used by all the patients when they are not retired to their individual cubicles for sleeping or disciplinary separation. The staff quarters and the office are walled off with a counter and glass partition, similar to a doctor's waiting room. As is the case every morning, about a dozen of the more lucid patients, including McMurphy, are seated in a semi-circle facing nurse Ratched as they go through some mental exercises. The remaining folks are aimlessly wandering in the background, engaged in various bizarre behaviors.

A very prim and properly starched Nurse Ratched is making some general comments, when McMurphy, looking very bored and spurred on by a timid fellow inmate, raises his hand and is recognized by Ratched. "Nurse Ratched, Martini is right there is another game today and we would like to watch it." With a look of exasperation reflecting her impatience with McMurphy's history of disruption, Nurse Ratched replies, "Well, Mr. McMurphy that would be alright if a majority of the patients would like to do that." McMurphy smiles broadly and says, "So can we take a vote?" and then continues without a pause and announces, "All right, raise your hands, which one of you nuts wanna watch the World Series?"

A Man On a Different Mission

R.P locks in a laser-like focus on one goal. He can be characterized as a man on a mission. He puts his hand up high and looks around the circle seeking followers. One by one, the hands of his band of brothers go up. At first, the hands go up tentatively, but then, when there is no retribution, more aggressively.

McMurphy's face is lighting up at the thought of victory. "All right, then," he says with exuberance, "we're going to watch the Series!" Nurse Ratched looks around calmly and, clearly savoring the moment, says "I only see nine hands." R.P. retorts, "Nine, only nine, why that's a landslide!" His smile gets even broader, but then it is Ratched's turn for a self-satisfied look. "There are eighteen men on the ward, Mr. McMurphy, and you have only nine votes; the motion fails," she declares with finality.

McMurphy looks around the room at the very dysfunctional group that remains. "All right, I only need one more vote right?" he asks with growing and obvious desperation. Ratched replies, "Yes that's right." With this, R.P. goes around the room, sadly trying to convince catatonic inmates and delusional patients to join in the vote. He does this with the creativity of a great salesman trying to bring the others around to his point of view, but all of this occurs without avail. While McMurphy is caught up in these futile activities, the meeting is breaking up and men are dispersing. Then, someone points out that the huge Native American inmate has his hand raised with a blank look on his face, and McMurphy lets out a yelp and declares, "The chief votes 'yes,' we have the votes!"

By this time, Nurse Ratched has gone back behind the glass partition, and R.P. taps on the glass and asks permission to turn the TV on for the Series. Nurse Ratched, by way of refusal, informs him that the meeting was over when the last vote was cast and, therefore, there will be no Series. McMurphy throws a mini-tantrum and slumps into a chair in front of the blank TV screen. The rest of the men are returning to their cubicles. McMurphy begins to stare at the blank screen and then suddenly becomes animated. He begins to announce the game as if he is watching it being played on the screen. He sounds like a professional announcer as he loudly, but carefully and in great detail, describes the pitcher winding up and delivering the pitch. The hit of the man at bat and the activities that follow on the field are similarly described in a booming announcer-like voice.

McMurphy's enthusiasm rises with his voice, and it is clear that he is enjoying the game. Intrigued by the hubbub, the men begin to come back into the room and gather around the TV and take an active role in the fantasy. They begin to cheer with each pitch and result. They are cheering and shouting, with R.P in the middle getting more exuberant with each pitch, as the camera goes to Nurse Ratched who bears the disgusted expression of someone who has just been defeated.

This scene is full of lessons about some of the qualities of leadership. It is clear, for example, that the leadership here does not depend on formality or rank. It is like the Good Samaritan at the jammed intersection who leaves his or her car and begins to direct traffic to break the gridlock. It is informal leadership, but leadership, nonetheless, that is at work, and this kind of leadership can often be observed. Some leaders have their roles thrust upon them, others seek out their positions of leadership, and still others—like McMurphy—wrest it from designated leaders in a battle for control.

While the focus here has been on McMurphy, there is much to be learned from an exploration of the Ratched character as well. With the limited qualities she possesses, she manages the ward well, but she leads it poorly. Nurse Ratched is, in fact, an excellent example of the difference between a manager and a leader. She possesses the qualities that are required for managerial success. She is knowledgeable about her task, has the requisite certifications for her position, displays talent at organizational skill and systems management and is confident in her abilities. With all of that, she exhibits no passion for her work, has no ability to inspire, and her manipulative demeanor often causes her integrity to be called into question. She can control the men on the ward, but she cannot begin to lead them. She cannot lead simply because, as every employee instinctively knows, leadership is about so much more than control. A named leader who relies upon title alone to achieve adherence to the rules will not be successful. Such an individual, who makes little attempt to consider motivational challenges or individual personalities, can not lead effectively. Nurse Ratched is a superb lesson in what not to do to succeed as a leader.

An Unlikely Setting for Leadership

McMurphy, on the other hand, shows great passion, creativity and compassion for his fellow inmates, all of which combine to give him his ability to inspire. He has charm, affability and approachability, traits which have others seeking him out for leadership. All of this is true, notwithstanding the dysfunctional environment in which McMurphy finds himself. Even with his relatively high level of mental capability, he may not be able to lead the men to realize a shared vision, but he can take them to some limited success. R. P. McMurphy, of course, is not the poster-child for leadership. His style and approach leave much to be desired in the search for leadership skills. But an examination of his character and the role that he plays demonstrates that leadership qualities can be found even in the most unlikely places.

The most important specific lesson to be learned from all of this is the quality and degree of focus which is personified in

McMurphy. Effective leaders must have the ability to sharply focus on the mission and the targets that are part of their particular leadership challenges. Esoteric notions of mission that are not sharp or are not clearly communicated are destined to lead to the mission's failure. A leader who hovers at the 50,000-foot level and leads with a "big picture" style can be effective only by descending to ground level on a regular basis to walk the spaces and get a "feel" for the situation. A high-level view combined with a generalized description of mission is a prescription for mediocrity. In fact, a 50,000-foot leader who never descends and still succeeds is probably not really leading, but only being dragged by his followers, or by circumstances, to success.

Using the "Common Enemy"

As well as being a requirement for true leadership, focus has universal application. All projects, all processes and all challenges will be faced with at least one common enemy. Leaders and their followers often gravitate toward a focus on the common enemy. This truism is at the heart of *One Flew Over The Cuckoo's Nest*. McMurphy wins many battles because of the common enemy in the person of Nurse Ratched. The American author Gene Fowler put it well when he wrote, "Everyone needs a warm personal enemy...to keep him free of rust in the movable parts of his mind." Ratched certainly kept R.P.'s mind free of rust as he focused on her, and the prospect of defeating the common enemy caused the troops to coalesce into a team.

Nurse Ratched is, in fact, the common enemy of one and all. She is the natural enemy of the patients by definition; she is a potential enemy of her subordinates who are dependent on her conduct; and, because she is lacking in so many leadership skills, she becomes the enemy of everyone with whom she comes into contact. McMurphy had an easy time wresting leadership from Ratched because she had become the common enemy.

Not all projects or processes are blessed with such an easily identifiable common enemy, but all have their unique challenges and leadership opportunities. Savvy leaders often harness the potentially unifying nature of these challenges and opportunities and cultivate the notion of them as a common enemy. Indeed, the leader may never formally identify the common enemy or call it by that name. McMurphy never announces, "It's us against Ratched!" But he does make use of the insight that all of the patients are locked in a battle with their controlling nurse and uses it in his strategy to appropriate leadership. By building their mission strategy to some degree around the enemy, people find a rallying point which helps them to focus their energies on the mission at hand.

A common enemy can actually provide the focus. But what happens if there is no Nurse Ratched type that a leader can target? The enemy is out there somewhere, and it need not be animate. General Eisenhower had the Nazis as an enemy, but in the weeks leading up to D-Day the common enemy became the terrible weather that hindered the launching of the offensive. Like the weather in the war effort, inanimate objects regularly serve as the enemy. Often the common enemy for a project is the schedule. And what project large or small doesn't have a budget issue? Meeting or beating the schedule and staying within budget are clear challenges around which everyone can rally for success.

There will be occasions when unlikely enemies are selected. The client is, by definition, a friend. After all, it was the customer that gave you the job, presumably when a competitor could have been selected. On occasion, though, the customer can be the "enemy" that provides the rallying point for success. For example, a leader can rally the troops by explaining that this customer is an inordinate stickler for response time and, therefore, everyone needs to focus on instant and massive response to the customer's needs. The strategy and tactics of executing the job can be designed to address the needs of the customer, and the job performers can focus on, and take pride in, exceeding the customer's expectations.

In the scene depicted in the film, the focus on the common enemy had a variety of results. When McMurphy sees his support by a show of hands, you can see the patients thinking of the consequence of their votes. The camera shows them looking first at R.P. and then back to Nurse Ratched, gauging what her reaction might be if they vote with their fellow inmates. Slowly, each takes comfort in the vote of the previous raised hand, and momentum begins to build. When faced with defeat at the first interpretation of the vote, the protagonist proceeds, undaunted, to gain additional support. In this way, he uses the group focus to build confidence and gain allegiance from the others. They know that R.P. will not give up and let them waste the votes he asked for. They see his creativity as he seeks additional support by relating to each potential ally on a very personal level. In this way, he also shows respect for those from whom he seeks support and, again, maintains the focus of the group. It is because of these behaviors that the tide begins turning against the unnamed, but clear, common enemy.

For her part, Nurse Ratched plays into the hands of our hero and becomes increasingly more transparent in her bias that propels her to try to doom McMurphy to a public humiliating failure. If McMurphy's key attribute is his ability to focus on the right thing, Ratched is his polar opposite. She has focus, but at every turn she focuses on the wrong thing. Instead of focusing on attaining the respect of her wards, she focuses on beating Mr. McMurphy. It is not lost on the observers that she comes off like a bully because she has all the weapons and is seen to be picking on an unarmed opponent. As a leader, she could have selected a suitable common enemy for her wards to focus upon, but instead she allowed herself to become the enemy.

No Paranoia

At the pinnacle of the scene, R.P., in his rendition of the announcer, is at his creative leadership best. With his unparalleled display of dedication to mission, his passion is amplified, and the challenge he is mounting for leadership control becomes evident. One by one, and this time without a glance at the enemy, the individuals emerge to join McMurphy in his fantasy baseball game. They focus on what their new leader is focusing on, and they believe what he is selling. As he cheers the fictitious plays, everyone cheers in unison. With one unified eruption of cheering, they transcend individualism and morph together into a single being. They evolve into a team unified against one common enemy, and this is another lesson to be learned.

The identification of a common enemy can turn individuals into a team. All leaders know the power of a team versus a group of individuals, and one aspect of successful leadership is the ability to identify a "common enemy" and, at least partially, to build the mission around that enemy.

Oh, and don't be paranoid about it!

GLORY
Courage

"His Brother's Keeper"

The War Between the States was the most horrific war ever engaged in by the people of this country. It produced more casualties, more dead, more physical devastation upon our land and more psychological conflict than all of the other wars that we have engaged in combined. At the battle of Antietam Creek alone, 35,000 American lives were lost, more than six times the number lost on D Day and more than ten times the number in more than two years in Iraq. The Civil War was a monumental clash of ideas and of people that consumed this nation for half a decade, with vestiges that continue to this day.

We know from history books and the millions of other words written to dissect, describe and interpret the events and causes of that conflict that slavery was only one element leading to its commencement. It is, nonetheless, true that slavery has always been central to any realistic interpretation of what caused the North and the South to take up arms, one against the other.

From W.D. Griffith's *Birth of a Nation*, which praised the Ku Klux Klan, to *Gone With the Wind*, which romanticized the old South, filmmakers have mined this historically rich era to bring it to life on the screen. The battles which are well-documented, Gettysburg, Antietam Creek, Bull Run and Harper's Ferry, to name a few, have been stylized for filmgoers' consumption. So, too, the bio-epics of the leaders who played pivotal roles in the war have

35mm immortality. Among the most notable of these leaders are Grant, Sherman, Lee and, of course, Lincoln. Even Custer has been immortalized in the film *They Died with Their Boots On*, which recounts his Civil War heroics in leading the 7th Calvary before his well-known last stand at Little Big Horn.

There is only one film of note which chronicles the exploits of the 54th Massachusetts regiment, the first all-black infantry unit in the Union Army. That film, *Glory*, is an historically accurate portrait of the formation, training and activation of the unit it portrays. It is a uniquely American story which offers to students of leadership an abundance of opportunities to examine what makes a leader great. It would be easy to suggest that the film teaches us to value diversity, but that observation would be tantamount to picking the very low-hanging fruit. In fact, the hero of the movie proves time and again that he is nearly colorblind when it comes to the challenge of leading his men, and his lack of bigotry is the most obvious of his desirable traits. Yet, there are more complex qualities to be discerned, among them courage, which is the focus of this chapter.

Courage is always counted as a necessary ingredient for successful leaders. Films which track courageous behavior are usually axiomatic, in the sense that just showing up at the battle would, in and of itself, be seen by most of us as a sound display of courage. Films like *Saving Private Ryan*, for example, are full of scenes that tell the tale of courageous actions. The fruit of what we can learn of leadership from this type of combat film is not even low-hanging—it's on the ground waiting to be scooped up. *Glory* has been selected from all the possible war pictures that could have been used for the many complex lessons that it offers.

Glory opens by telling us that the film is based, in part, on the letters of the commanding officer of the 54th Massachusetts Regiment, which became known as the Swamp Angels. The insights offered by these letters give us a rare perspective into the motives and thinking of *Glory's* hero. The story begins by following our hero into his first big battle, sans the 54th, at Antietam Creek. We watch him as a young captain when he is wounded and sent home to recuperate, having experienced the horrors of war up close and personal. We see him as a young man of refined manners with a privileged upbringing in the company of a prominent family and influential friends. Perhaps there is some theatrical license taken when the camera captures his meeting with Fredrick Douglas, probably the most renowned black leader in America at the time. It is at this very same meeting that the captain is told that he has been proposed as the commander of the first all-Negro army unit that is about to be formed. He is all of 27 years old.

Maturing Sense of Leadership

The rest of the film depicts the evolution of the unit and the maturation of its commander, Robert Gould Shaw. During the growth of both the unit and Shaw, there are several scenes in which his courage is key, and the three most compelling will be explored here.

Robert Gould Shaw was, as noted, of the manor born. He likely owed his first commission to the influence of his Boston Brahmin parents, and most certainly their rank in society was what prompted his promotion to the rank of colonel and his subsequent selection as commander of the new regiment. From the outset, however, it is clear that Shaw takes his promotion and mission very seriously. His actions bespeak a belief that his mission is to train the men under his command for combat; and, unlike those around him, he believes in the men and their potential. While Shaw and his men are looked down upon by his peers and by other white soldiers, he is almost naïve in his perception of his men and his mission. He seems to assume that his task has no more or less the degree of difficulty than the command of any group of soldiers.

It is early in the training process that Shaw's courage and his own evolving maturity are initially exhibited. While on routine patrol, Shaw's men capture what appears to be a deserter and, by way of punishment, Shaw publicly flogs the miscreant. Later, Shaw learns that the man was not deserting but was, instead, searching the surrounding area for boots, since neither footwear nor uniforms had yet been issued. This leads to Shaw's discovery that many of his men are suffering from foot injuries and blisters, because their shoes are ill-fitting or they have no shoes, something of which Shaw, whose boots and uniforms were tailor-made, was naively unaware.

Upon the advice of his master sergeant, Shaw sets out to get a supply of footwear through the normal channels. He personally puts in a written requisition for the needed equipment. By way of reply, the quartermaster informally sends Shaw a message inferring that the standard-issue boots had to go to the fighting troops and, thus, his men will not receive such luxuries. The unsaid, but obvious, racial overtones were not lost on our young hero. With some of his men in tow, Shaw marches to the supply building where, leaving his men outside, he storms through the door, enraged by the thought that his men will be treated differently than others. It is significant that Shaw leaves his men outside, because his motive is not to impress them but to accomplish a mission.

The startled quartermaster inquires about the nature of Shaw's visit and, when informed of the young commander's purpose, says with a smile, "I told you that we have no boots for your men." Shaw hesitates for a moment and begins smashing cups and trays on the shelves closest to him. He towers over the seated quartermaster and, growing more red-faced, he shouts, "I am a colonel you little cuss. You think you can keep 700 union soldiers without proper shoes because you think it's funny? Where does that power come from?" With that, Shaw demands the shoes. And he gets them.

Courage, Reinforced by Success

This was to be Shaw's first test of courage. He passed it with flying colors, and his courage was bolstered by the success. Up until this time, Shaw had displayed some small degree of courage in his everyday duties only by facing down subordinates in his own company and standing firm when challenged by his own executive officer. As he employs his courage to get the much-needed shoes for his men, however, Shaw's journey that will lead to his ultimate act of courage commences. From that day forward, he and his men are growing together.

Not everyone was taken with Shaw's small successes. His regiment was continually called upon to do menial and strenuous tasks, such as road-clearing and deforesting wooded areas, while the longed-for prospect of combat remained bleak. When his regiment was finally selected to join another Negro squad to raid the village of Darien, Georgia, Shaw went along in excited anticipation of a skirmish. He was sorely disappointed when a colleague leading both of the units began to speak disparagingly of the Negro unit led by Shaw, and his disappointment turned to shock when his colleague's Negro soldiers were turned loose, like hounds to the fox, to pillage the town. As the soldiers set about their random lawlessness and the harassment of the town's women, behaving generally like so much rabble, Shaw's well-trained and disciplined troops were aghast at what they were witnessing. For their part, they remained in ranks waiting commands.

When the officer in charge ordered Shaw to have his men set the houses ablaze, Shaw's courage was called to task again. Shaw steeled himself and told the officer, "No sir, I will not have my men obey an immoral order." Shaw and his men awaited the response. "Colonel, I have given you a direct order and you will obey it, or I will have you taken away and I will take command of your men," came the most unambiguous reply. Rather than have his men subjected to the rule of this madman, thus ruining everything he and the men had worked for, Shaw complied, and his men carried out the order.

Here is the conundrum for our young leader Shaw: Should he challenge the authority of the field commander and hope for victory in a court martial, or should he swallow the urge to best this sorry excuse for a leader and follow the immoral order to advance a superior cause? Is this another case where discretion is truly the better part of valor? This scene is important for what it instructs students of leadership.

Shaw had thus far succeeded in leading his men to achievements well beyond their wildest aspirations. The contrast of his men to the men under his colleague's leadership was stark indeed. Yet, both groups of men were behaving as they were expected to behave, albeit with very different outcomes. Shaw had high expectations of the men under his command, higher even than they had for themselves, and the men were inspired to live up to Shaw's view of them. He was unwilling to sacrifice the hard-earned growth that had been achieved as a result for a personal principle.

On your own leadership journey, you may find yourself in a similar dilemma. Looking at the situation in which Shaw found himself, it is easy for the casual observer to take issue with his decision. Some might suggest that one should never relinquish a personal principle. An argument can even be advanced that if you surrender your principles, you surrender your right to lead. Of course, in life, as in the movie, the dilemma may be occasioned by competing principles, and the solution to the predicament may often be less clear than you would like. Indeed, in Shaw's situation the principle of avoiding immoral acts might have been seen by him as a bright line, a line he didn't want to cross. Turning over his men may have even risked sacrificing more than just a single principle. However, he had insight enough to recognize, and give priority to, the competing principle of loyalty to his men.

It would be convenient to have all of our principles so clearly and unambiguously defined as not to have to make difficult decisions, but, of course, the role of a leader is not so uncomplicated. There will, in fact, be many difficult decisions that require not only courage to choose what should be the controlling principle but some measure of judgment as well. To be sure, courage must be exercised along with good judgment, which was looked at in-depth in the context of another classic film, *12 Angry Men*.

After Shaw's own watershed decision, he continues to mature as the film's story continues to play out. His men are now bound together by their shared adversity and respect for Shaw's leadership; and Shaw, for his part, comes to recognizes that leadership is more than just leading his men. He discovers that leadership is taking command of his own circumstances when others thwart his progress, as in the footwear incident. He also knows, through the experience of the ransacking incident, that principles are complex and often in conflict with one another. You may, yourself, be in a situation where you are "damned if you do and damned if you don't," but a choice will have to be made. And effective leaders do just that.

As he moves forward, Shaw's sole remaining ambition is to be ordered into combat, but he continues to be rebuffed at every turn in his attempt to build an organization that is invited to do battle. Finally, the young leader takes matters into his own hands. Once again, he forces a confrontation with the regional commanding officer, who is less serving and more self-serving as a leader, and suggests that if he is not given a combat assignment he may go to the war department and expose the nefarious activities that have been engaged in by the commander. His threat is successful in that the officer orders the unit into combat. In this, Shaw may have been well-advised to have been careful what he wished for.

The final scene now begins to unfold. Thousands of troops are gathering on the beaches around Charleston, South Carolina. As the camera pans the beautiful ocean horizon, it stops at a view of Fort Wagner, which is in marked contrast to the beauty of the sea and the rising sun. The General who commands the entire force is seen briefing the assembled regiment leaders, including our protagonist. The commanding General explains the situation in the gravest terms. He describes in detail the nature of the fort's defenses, including the thousand rebels who are committed to its protection, and the cannons and physical barriers which have been erected to hinder the breaching of the sand walls. The General continues by laying out his attack strategy, which includes, for lack of an alternative, the necessity for a frontal attack. He announces that one regiment will be required to lead the attack.

The officer makes it abundantly clear that the leading regiment will doubtless suffer great losses in making the initial break and keeping the enemy occupied while the other regiments attack through the breach.

Fight or Flight

The gravity of the situation is not lost on the gathered commanders. One of them, Robert Gould Shaw, steps forward and announces, "General, sir, the 54th Massachusetts request the honor of leading the charge on Fort Wagner." The General looks stunned and replies, "Your men have not had any sleep for two days. Are you sure they are up to this?" A close-up of our now fully-matured hero reveals a quivering chin as he thoughtfully responds, "There is more to fighting than rest sir. There is character, there is strength of heart. You should have seen these men in battle two days ago; they were a sight to behold. We'll be ready, sir. When do you want us?"

The rest, as they say, is history. The 54th Massachusetts Regiment, aka the Swamp Angels, led the charge to the thunderous cheers of the white regiments who lined up to see them march off. The respect inherent in the cheers had been well-earned by the brave men about to do combat. Regrettably, though they did their job superbly, the assault was as devastating as predicted by the commanding General. More than half of the 54th was lost in the attack. Robert Gould Shaw was among them. It may lead you to ask, what was Colonel Shaw thinking when he volunteered?

No doubt the quality of courage was never more forcefully on display then when Shaw stepped forward to "request the honor" of volunteering. The consequences of his actions were easy to predict. He was certain that his charges would suffer significant losses in the attack. He must have understood that his own death was nearly certain. Biblically, it might have been said best with the phrase, "Greater love hath no man but to lay down his life for another." In reality, the greatest evidence of courage comes when a person knowingly takes some action that places his own life in significant jeopardy. Other displays of courage pale by comparison.

Had Shaw no fear? On the contrary, he was certainly afraid. General Foch, commander of the French forces in World War I, reprimanded one of his officers when he found out that the officer disciplined one of his men for showing fear in battle. Foch admonished the officer by saying that, "None but a coward dares to boast that he has never known fear." Shaw was not a coward.

Colonel Shaw's short military career was a condensed version of the development of a leader. It is the compression of that development that gives the film its power and allows it to serve as the best example, among the scores of war films that could have been chosen, to illustrate courage. Here is a leader who was thrust into leadership, certainly ill-prepared from the perspective of training and experience. Fortunately, Shaw was blessed with a strong character and sense of self that allowed him to survive the rigors of leadership, and he was able to use his "on-the-job" training to fill in the gaps in his formal training.

Was Shaw born with the courage gene, or did he develop the quality while facing the exigencies of war? There will be further examination of the nature vs. nurture aspects of leadership in later chapters, but suffice to say that the courage we see displayed by Shaw in *Glory* suggests that both factors were at work. As with many qualities of leadership, you or others may be born with a certain leaning in favor of a particular leadership quality, but it will be the course of events and your response to them that brings out the essence of the quality.

Heart Versus Head

Shaw was challenged to lead a group of men who had major self-esteem issues, to say the least. After all, these were men who were recently slaves and considered property. Shaw knew that these men felt that they had much to prove to themselves and to the others who were watching and making judgments about the unit. As a leader, Shaw himself was challenged by multiple factors. He had the normal challenge of shaping recruits and volunteers into a disciplined fighting force, exacerbated by the very complex issues connected with race and slavery and the social and economic landscape. Shaw was very sensitive to his challenge and was torn between his inclination to revert to his privileged past and his equally strong tendency to feel empathy and compassion for his charges.

Shaw fought for the assignment to go into combat, not because he had an aggressive personality. He fought his natural tendencies, because all evidence, including his letters, shows him to be a gentle, cultured man. He knew his men needed validation of their worth. He chose to volunteer on a nearly suicidal mission, not to satisfy a death wish, but because he had a sense of history and the place his men would have in that history if they could succeed at this very public endeavor under the spotlight of the press and other regiments. Shaw viewed the challenges he faced as opportunities and, in doing so, the courage he displayed was as pure and as selfless as can be depicted on film or in reality.

Leaders are often faced with challenges and opportunities which require courage. Timidity is not a quality that serves leaders well. That is not to say that recklessness or foolhardiness will advance a leader's cause. Neither this film in particular nor the study of leadership in general should counsel you in favor of irrational decisions that are made in furtherance of the machismo-like tendencies of some leaders. Rather, you should regard this film as a chance to consider how conflicting factors can interact and challenge a leader's courage to do the right thing. Of course, this story has major implications about diversity and American culture that overlay the turmoil experienced by Shaw in carrying out his mission and that offer something to be learned as well.

Whether played out against a backdrop of huge social implications, as it was for Shaw, or within the confines of a power project in Iowa or elsewhere, having courage, which includes having the courage of one's own convictions, is exceedingly important in the pursuit of leadership excellence.

THE GODFATHER
Self-Control

"Cool Hand Vito"

It goes without saying that there is nothing about organized crime that should be emulated. Under the "cool" exterior of a Tony Soprano character of the television drama or real-life hoods like Gotti and Gravano lies a ruthless thug who uses violence and mayhem to achieve his ends. But the beauty of studying leadership qualities, rather than leaders, is that it offers the possibility of looking at qualities in a broad range of characters in fact and fiction.

Many characters that lend themselves to a study of leadership qualities are not good leaders; in fact, many are not even good people and may not be the least entitled to our approval or affection. But, as with the Godfather and his role in the world of organized crime, we look at these figures for what they can instruct about some discrete aspect of leadership. Here, it's the "organized" piece that warrants study and not the "crime" piece. Whatever might be said about this film, and it is surely a great cinematic accomplishment at that, *The Godfather* epic is noteworthy in its skill at portraying the specific leadership qualities that enable Don Corleone's success within his world. Disregarding the illegitimacy of his enterprises, his leadership skills are indisputable.

The Godfather is one of the most-watched films of all time. It portrays the life of Don Vito Corleone, the head of one of the five mafia families in New York. We observe his evolution from a timid immigrant arriving at Ellis Island to an old man who dies in the tomato garden on his New York estate. Throughout, the central character is the consummate teacher. His three sons, his trusted lieutenants, and even his enemies are inundated with the lessons he delivers on family values, trust, loyalty, courage, focus, resoluteness and the importance of setting an example, to name a few of his subjects. Always teaching, he is in this regard the epitome of a mentor, and he takes the job seriously. While the quality we will focus on in this chapter is self-control, I commend this film to anyone with an interest in how particular qualities allow individuals to succeed at their roles. This film and its sequels, enjoyable for many other reasons as well, are worthwhile for the forceful depiction of the various qualities that propelled the don to success as the leader of a crime family.

Even with the catholicity of viewing audiences, it is worth providing a trailer of sorts concerning this epic. However else it is viewed, *The Godfather* is a family story. It tells of the life and death of Vito Corleone, olive oil importer and distributor. He has a nuclear family with a loyal and subservient wife who bore him three sons and a daughter. He also has an extended family, of the organized crime variety, which he tends to with equal seriousness and effort. His eldest and youngest sons, Santino and Michael respectively, are the primary targets for most of his lessons. The effect of these lessons is that Michael becomes a tintype of his father, albeit a reluctant one, while Santino constantly requires remedial attention.

At the beginning of this family story, we are introduced to Don Vito Corleone, his title bestowed upon him after he ascended to the top of the crime family, at the apex of his personal and professional power. Having amassed great wealth and influence and, most importantly, the respect of his family, extended family and underworld competitors, he concerns himself with his legacy and the tending of his flock. To him, it's all a matter of respect.

A Blend of Gandhi and Patton

I found it fascinating that the fictional character depicted in *The Godfather* has so many of the leadership traits of both the gentle Gandhi and the gruff Patton—respect, courage and mentoring ability among them. Perhaps Mario Puzo fashioned his leader after these and other men of note.

The opening scene is profound in its condensation of what is fundamental in the story that is about to unfold. Don Corleone's wealth is obvious from the splendor to be seen in his compound and the lavishness of the festivities for the very special event that is taking place. The scene is the celebration of his only daughter's wedding day, a day on which, by custom, the Godfather provides an audience for all those seeking his services. He is seen attentively listening as a humble funeral director implores him to avenge the brutal rape of his daughter by killing the perpetrators.

The Don listens with obvious empathy but demurs, explaining that this is not justice that the funeral director seeks, for his daughter was not killed. The Godfather expresses surprise that the requester expects him to "do murder." Don Corleone takes the time to admonish the man in the view and hearing of the others in the room. He explains that he is saddened that, even though they have known each other for decades, this is the first time the undertaker has sought the aid of the Don. Vito chides him by reminding him that he now knows that he cannot rely on the police for protection or justice, let alone vengeance. He expresses disappointment that until now, until this time of need, the petitioner has not embraced what the Godfather represents. After the undertaker acknowledges his blunders and the resulting slight, the Godfather agrees to mete out just punishment and prophetically informs the director that someday he, the Godfather, may need the director's services. As the funeral director makes his exit, the Godfather turns to his consigliore, his trusted counsel and implementer, and directs that the "job" be given to people who will not "get carried away." He ends the directive with his view that "After all we are not animals."

The essence of the Don's leadership style is established in this scene, and the impression that we get is buttressed in almost every scene that follows. He is cool and calm in the face of the passion and emotion of others. He does not gloat over his ability to humble the man who would seek his help. In all of this, Vito Corleone epitomizes the quality of self-control, the difficulty of which was best put by Aristotle in his treatise on ethics: "It is easy to become angry. But to be angry with the right person, to the right degree, at the right time, for the right purpose, and in the right way...this is not easy."

Clear Expectations, Clear Directions

The Godfather himself is teaching a lesson as he uses his power to resolve a problem in the right way, in the "just" way and with the right amount of resources. While he is forgiving in a sense, willing to leave the perpetrators of the rape with their lives, he is clear about his expectations and his plan. As the scene continues, the Godfather repeats this approach and reinforces the underlying principle: the right remedy at the right time and place.

In his next challenge, he is confronted with a baker whose potential son-in-law has an immigration problem. The nature of the issue reminds us that the Don not only has the power over the underworld but also has influence in the legitimate world. This problem the Godfather resolves by instructing his consigliore to "Give this to one of the Jew councilmen."

Finally, the Don hears the woes of his own godson, a famous singer, who needs a part in a film to turn his career around. Showing us the layers of his style, the Godfather slaps his godson when he whines about his trouble, and, with a loud voice but a controlled temper, the Don tells him to "Be a man!" After inquiring of his godson if he spends time with his family, the Godfather gets back to business and asks for the name of the person who can make the final decision on the movie role; he predicts that his godson will soon get the part. His instructions to his aide this time include, "See this big shot and reason with him." Few who have seen this movie can forget the horse's head that is a part of the "reasoning."

The panoply of leadership qualities depicted in the opening scene is often repeated in the remainder of the film. The Godfather is attentive, decisive, steady, confident, insightful, creative and unflappable. He is also, at times, organized, knowledgeable and reasoned. These skills are all employed by the title character in this brief but powerful scene, and they set the stage for much of what follows.

As with many possessed of one quality or the other, the Godfather is in no small measure a product of his youth. Vito Corleone was left fatherless at the hands of the Mafia wars in the old country. He is hidden by his family from his father's murderers and is sent to America as a boy. Here, steeped in a strong family ethic and internal fortitude, he rises to the top of a competitive environment dominated by the underworld. He thrives in that world, where loyalty and courage are rewarded on a quid pro quo basis.

Control Plus

Of all of the qualities that Vito Corleone exhibits, the one that seems most worthy of our attention in the exploration of what makes a leader is the quality of self-control. It is a quality that is well-learned by his youngest son but notably absent in his other offspring. Fredo and Connie are never trusted with important family issues, Fredo because he is mentally challenged and Connie because she is a female. Both of them are devoid of self-control, a failing that ultimately leads to Fredo's betrayal of Michael and that is reflected in Connie's life of disastrous relationships, unhappy marriages and degradation. By contrast, the three main characters, Vito, Santino and Michael, benefit from their ability to exercise self-control.

It is axiomatic that you are the only person you can ever hope to consistently control. You may have some control over others for some fleeting periods of time, but you have the ability to control yourself all the time. And the degree to which you succeed in your control of yourself is likely to be directly related to the degree to which you are able to control or lead others. *The Godfather* offers some clear examples of self-control that contribute to the understanding of this phenomenon.

Vito Corleone is, of course, the dominant central character around which the film is based and, as has been noted, he is constantly in a mentoring role. "Do you spend time with your family?" he asks his godson; "A man who does not spend time with his family is not a man to be respected." While these remarks are directed to his godson in one of the opening scenes, the message he is sending is also meant for his son Santino and his consigliore, Tom Hagan, who are also present. Later in the film, a meeting is arranged with a rival crime family. Accompanied by his leadership team, the Godfather affords respect to the head of the rival family, a known drug dealer, but turns down a proffered lucrative partnership. Santino interrupts this discussion to give voice to his incredulity at the Godfather's decision, which prompts another lesson after the meeting. After making sure everyone on his team is present, the Godfather speaks loudly, but with control, when he admonishes Sonny, "Never tell a man what you are thinking, it shows weakness." To the Don, Santino's outburst was a reflection of a lapse in control. More then just teaching with words, the Don walks this talk. He repeatedly leads by example and, most importantly, shows the consistency of his qualities even when his guard is down. Not all of his children are possessed of this same control or the same consistency.

Paying the Price

Santino "Sonny" Corleone is the eldest son and heir-apparent to the Don. He is renowned for his courage and fighting ability. As shown in the drug dealer scene, he has a problem with control, and there are cracks in the armor with regard to his ability to control his libido as well as his temper. These flaws are best depicted in his last scene in the film, when he pays the ultimate price for his loss of self-control.

Michael Corleone is the youngest of the clan and the cleanest in terms of his involvement in crime. In many ways, he is also the most complex of the characters. He is a war hero who has no interest in the "family business." He is a man of courage and integrity who seems to be the antithesis of what the family epitomizes. His differences are highlighted when he joins the Marines. He makes this decision without counsel and is undeterred by an angry Sonny, who derides him because "This war is not about the family." As Michael tells his girlfriend in the opening segment, after regaling her with gruesome stories of his father's exploits and seeing the shock on her face, "That's my family Kay, it's not me."

So, what is the role of self-control as the film unfolds? In the film, as in the life of leaders in all fields, it is adversity which brings out the need for self-control, and it is in trying times that its importance can best be observed. Controlling oneself is easy in routine times. It is under pressure, and often amidst chaos, that self-control is most difficult and most valuable. These kinds of challenges to self-control unfold in three defining scenes in *The Godfather.*

In the first, Michael has just returned to the family home with a broken jaw inflicted by a corrupt cop who was trying to finish off the Don after a botched assassination attempt. In the room are the leaders of the family business, including Tom Hagen, Santino, and Tessio and Clemenza who serve as family capos or captains. Tempers are running high, and Santino, acting in the place of his incapacitated father, is trying to figure out what to do with the threat presented by the rogue cop and the notorious drug dealer, both of whom are sponsored by the rival family responsible for the assignation attempt. "So what are we gonna do with the cop, eh? We can't kill him, no one has ever done that, and we would lose the loyalty of the other families and our allies in politics. What are we gonna do?"

The camera focuses on Michael and begins a very slow dolly that draws closer as he speaks. "Who said you can't kill a cop? A corrupt cop, a cop who was on the take? We have reporters on the payroll don't we, Tom? They might like a story like that." The camera moves ever so slowly toward Michael as he formulates a detailed plan that will result in murder. "We set up a meeting with me somewhere where they feel safe. And if Clemenza can hide a gun for me to get it after they frisk me...I will kill them both." The group erupts into uncontrolled laughter. Sonny mocks Michael in a loving way, "What are you gonna do, you gotta get up real close, this isn't the army where you shot them from a mile away, you'll get blood all over your ivy-league suit!" He goes on to say, "You're taking this too personal, Mikey, too personal!" Michael never cracks a smile and coldly replies, "It's not personal Sonny, it's strictly business."

Keeping Your Head

Here, when others were paralyzed by emotion, Michael became the leader. Instead of begin overwhelmed by anger or rage, he calmly outlines a plan, a plan that could jeopardize his life or freedom. Kipling said it best, "When all around you are losing their heads and you can keep yours, you will become a man, my son." Michael not only kept his head, he revealed himself as his father's heir, the Godfather's protégé. His style was, of course, to differ from his father's. His skills at leading the family are similar to those of his mentor, but he would go on to apply them differently. He is, in his role as the head of the family, much colder and more driven by practicality, in contrast to his father's more compassionate and paternalistic approach. It is clear evidence that the same leadership skills can succeed when applied by different personalities. Calculated passion can be just as forceful as explosive passion; each is at its most effective when it comes from the heart.

The older brother and would-be heir had a different demeanor. We had a chance in the previous scene to see how Santino handles his anger. He publicly beats his brother-in-law to a bloody pulp after finding out he beat his sister. Later, while at home, he gets a call from Connie, who is screaming and crying as she tells Sonny how her husband has beaten her again. Sonny loses it and starts screaming at her to "Stay there, just stay there!" He slams the phone down, rushes past his bodyguards and heads out in his car to the toll road that will take him to avenge his sister. He is totally out of control. When he arrives at the toll station, he is hemmed in by his assassins and is graphically and brutally slain. In Sonny's case, his temper stripped him of his logic and rationality and cost him his life. Uncontrolled temper trumps reason, rationality and common sense and is the bane of wise decisions.

After Sonny meets his fate, the Godfather has his self-control tested. Vito Corleone has been recuperating from his near-fatal injuries suffered earlier, in the same home where Sonny has stormed out to his death. Tom Hagen is girding himself to break the news of Sonny's death, when Vito makes his way downstairs and sits beside Tom in the hall. The Godfather is obviously weak, and bandages hold his throat together. He sits opposite Tom and speaks with difficulty. "And so, my consigliore, do you want to tell me what everyone else seems to know?" With great hesitation Tom tells him, "Sonny was ambushed on the expressway, he is dead." The Godfather exhales deeply, as if the life has been taken from his body, and his anguished eyes are filled with tears as he murmurs, "I want no acts of violence. I want a meeting with the heads of the five families. This war ends now."

At what is arguably the most devastating moment in any parent's life, he reaches down and brings forth the quality that best serves his position of leadership, self-control. Tragedy steels him. He instinctively knows what all good leaders know, that it is in times of adversity and chaos that leaders must draw upon their inner strength and continue to lead.

For an ordinary leader, the loss of self-control may not cost lives. But it will certainly cost the confidence of those who are led. Where do you rank on the self-control scale? Do you revert to using profanity to express yourself? Do you slam things around and throw pens and the like when you get bad news? Do you storm out of meetings or dismiss underlings with a disdainful comment or gesture when you don't like what you hear? You know yourself better then anyone, and it's worth taking the time to evaluate your own self-control to see if you count it as a strength or a weakness.

Self-control is not about coolness or a lack of passion or compassion. It's about control. It might be described as the ability to see through the fog of confusion and to bring clarity to the situation. It is the effective leader who can keep a clear mind in the throes of crisis or tumult. A leader who keeps that clarity is often described as someone who can "cut through all the junk and get to the heart of the problem." In the final analysis, leaders who maintain self-control and who don't allow their talent to be diminished by the loss of control are positioning themselves for success.

Showing emotion or having a strong reaction can be a valuable tool so long as it doesn't signal the actual loss of self-control. Using the film as an example and recalling the Godfather's encounter with his godson, it's clear that Don Corleone did not slap his godson out of anger, but rather for effect. The Don was, in fact, very much in control. What is important is not so much whether your colleagues or competitors or others around you think that you have ever lost control; it's whether you actually were in control of what you were saying or doing at a given point in time. It is a common negotiation tactic to yell, slam a fist on the table or even walk out of the room for effect. Whether or not you regard tactics like that as legitimate or desirable, they are often the product of great self-control, not any lack of it. The objective is to achieve a particular outcome, and a show of emotion can often advance that cause.

Lose It and You Lose

In truth, the value of maintaining self-control cannot be overstated. In the business world, there are many variables. There are many elements, human and inanimate, which can impact a situation, a negotiation or a project plan, and no one can control all of the variables. As stated earlier, the only thing you can absolutely control is yourself and your actions.

In watching *The Godfather*, you will see many examples of self-control. The scene preceding the one with the head of the ill-fated horse has the lascivious movie mogul ranting and raving at Tom Hagen, insulting Tom and his employer, the Don. Tom slides his dinner plate away and quietly says, "Can you have the driver take me to the airport? My employer insists on hearing bad news immediately." With like equanimity, Michael never loses his head or his temper at his brother-in-law, Carlo, who was responsible for the death of Sonny. Instead, he quietly questions him and manipulates him into admitting culpability...and then calmly issues orders to have him killed. Even the hated drug dealer shows control when he gently tells Michael that the attempt on the Godfather's life was not personal, "It was only business."

Controlling yourself is your business. Like every other quality discussed in this book, it is a quality that you can foster. You can hone self-control, and you can develop and improve it.

There is one simple verity: you are being observed and measured each day. A friend of mine, a real life Vito, recently observed, "In today's world you can guarantee that you will be caught on film almost every day." Leaders should behave as though they are constantly on film. Your colleagues, your peers, those whom you lead or manage and those who manage or lead you are measuring you against all these qualities. They may not be measuring you formally, or even consciously, but they are measuring you. So, you need to be honestly and conscientiously evaluating yourself at the same time, all the time, to see how you are doing. As part of the process, watch *The Godfather*. Learn from the silver screen, as you focus on particular qualities and see them in action and witness the results.

WHAT'S IT ALL ABOUT?

In the Genes or In the Jeans?

From our earliest recollections, we have been confronted with leaders. Parents or parent figures certainly come to mind, and we may recall that one of them took on the role as the head of the house. Those of you who had puppies may be familiar with the alpha dog hierarchical animal structure, a model that relies on instinct, and perhaps breeding, to determine who leads and who follows in the canine world. We have also seen the circles of teens and pre-teens in their social and other environments. A leader always seems to emerge, a youngster to whom the others look for approval or direction. It isn't always, or even usually, the biggest one or the smartest one who emerges as the leader.

Examples of the emerging leader syndrome can be found in the films and their characters in this book and in other media as well. In *Of Mice and Men*, for example, Steinbeck is eloquent in describing the gentle giant who is led by his slight companion upon whom he depends for comfort, guidance and direction. In the *Dead End Kids*, a popular film series in the 1940's, the kids are led by a diminutive Muggsy, aka "Slip," who orders around a ragtag group of ruffians, many of whom are tougher and stronger than he is. These boys put up with verbal, and sometimes physical, abuse from their leader in an effort to curry his favor. You can watch reruns of *Happy Days, Dennis the Menace, Ozzie and Harriett,* even the *Three Stooges,* and each will further illustrate the point.

In another movie example, William Wallace of *Braveheart* fame is in every way an ordinary man who nevertheless ascends as leader of the Scots. Wallace makes this leap without election or formal designation. Unlike military leaders, coaches or bosses, Muggsy, Steinbeck's Lenny, and others like them have no title, no grant of power and no formal rank that invests them with the authority of leadership. So, how is it that they have come to be leaders? If you were but one of the followers in your high school or college coterie, are you forever doomed to looking to others for leadership? Do you have to wait to have offspring to have your time as a leader? Even then, might your leadership role be usurped by your spouse?

Inherited or Developed?

Leaders are born. Leaders are made. Both statements may be accurate. All leaders possess several of the qualities that are described in preceding chapters, some leaders may even have all of them, and it is an interesting exercise to examine individual leaders and try to determine what made the leadership of each a success. However, a more intriguing exercise than that is one that examines the qualities themselves to see how each comes to be. Psychologists, sociologists and armchair intellectuals have all long debated nature vs. nurture, environment vs. heredity, inborn vs. inbred. Ultimately, the debate centers on whether it is our genetics or our surroundings that have the greater influence on our personalities and our very identities.

The value of exploring this aspect of individual leadership qualities is that it can help you to shape the right approach, with a focus on education, experience or both, to enhance the qualities that may help *you* to develop. If you seek to hone qualities of leadership that can help you to succeed, you are apt to conclude, as I have, that some qualities can be learned, some can be developed over time and some are innate—you have them or you don't. I don't hold myself out as a psychologist or even an armchair intellectual. I have, however, had decades of leadership experience, and after carefully examining those leaders I have encountered, I have concluded that leaders are made, not born.

You can certainly become a more skilled leader by improving those qualities which are of most value to leadership. But you need to have some idea of which qualities are a part of your individual make-up—or not—and which can be learned or developed, so you can spend your time and energy changing those things that can really be changed. You know yourself better than anyone knows you, and you are the best judge of where you need to improve. You will be aided in the task of improving yourself if you spend your time where it will make a difference and in ways that will really result in your improvement. It is worth exploring a number of particular leadership qualities to better understand how your leadership profile might be enhanced.

As we look back at the various characters and how they are depicted in the films, we can see that the characters showed multiple leadership qualities in addition to the traits that were highlighted. The primary and secondary traits are worth reviewing with respect to whether or not they can be learned and developed or, indeed, if they are characteristics of birth. This second look will seek to identify those traits that lend themselves to being learned, those that are developed with time and experience, and those that are neither.

Put yourself in the picture now. How do you stack up against the qualities? How might you set forth a plan to improve your self-evaluation? Is it possible to learn or develop these attributes?

Key Leadership Traits That Can Be Developed

Inspiration. While there are certain inherent personality traits that make some individuals more inspiring than others, the ability to inspire others can be learned. The ability to inspire is basically the ability to motivate others, and few of you have not employed motivational skills. You may have simply motivated fellow workers to take a break and walk through the park. The same skills, more deftly applied, could motivate people to join our sheriff Will Kane in the formation of a posse. Anyone can read books on the subject of motivation, from the 1936 book by Dale Carnegie, *How to Win Friends and Influence People,* to the more recent and esoteric texts on the subject. And just about every course or conference that teaches presentation skills is, at its core, about motivation. The bottom line is that inspiring others is a learnable skill, one which any aspiring leader will need to succeed. When Will Kane in *High Noon* failed to inspire, he failed as a leader.

The great orchestra leader, Arturo Toscanini, once found himself unable to describe the effect he was looking for in a certain segment of Debussy's *La Mer.* After some thought, he took a silk handkerchief from his pocket and tossed it high into the air. The musicians watched the slow graceful descent of the silk cloth, and Toscanini smiled as it glided to the floor. "There," he said, "play it like that." That's what made Toscanini a great leader. His ability to reach the whole orchestra by reaching each section, indeed each musician, is legendary. The ability to inspire is perhaps the most basic of leadership skills in that, in order to lead, one must have followers, and it is the leader who motivates and inspires those followers.

Self-control. If you are not able to control yourself, you can hardly expect that you will be able to lead others. Fortunately, self-control can be learned, and the growing popularity of yoga and meditation suggests that increasing numbers of people are anxious to find ways to improve their discipline and self-control. Without any special learning, we've all forced ourselves to "count to ten" or "take a deep breath" or to simply think before we respond with some gut reaction. These are all exercises in learning self-control. Today's society is full of challenges that should sensitize us to the need for self-control. Road rage, on the one hand, and anger management classes on the other, are only two of many new phenomena which have invaded our culture as some people are driven to lose their self-control and others are seeking to regain it.

In many of the films which have been explored in this text, self-control, or its loss, is featured prominently. The loss of self-control by Patton in the soldier slapping incident is a good example. On several occasions, Erin Brockovich's loss of self-control gets in the way of her achieving her goals. The reverse is the case with the key juror in *12 Angry Men* and with Don Corleone, for whom the ability to keep their emotions in check allowed them to succeed. Leaders can learn self-control; and if they don't, they will soon learn that the loss of self-control can lead to failure.

Delegation. Delegation is a skill that can—and must—be learned. Leadership, by definition, cannot be exercised without delegation. "Empowerment" is the trendy word for giving others authority or assignments, but whether you call it empowerment, delegation, assignment or something else, you must be able to call on others for assistance to achieve your ends. Since no one can do it all alone, delegating is fundamental to a leader's success. In the discussion of *Erin Brockovich*, I noted that while Erin was well-versed in the skill, perhaps the art, of preparation, she left something to be desired in terms of being a good overall leader.

Erin lacked the ability to delegate and seemingly coveted all the tasks associated with success.

You will recall that in one of the scenes that is described, she expresses resentment about her boss's decision to get outside expert assistance, because she has little understanding of the concept of delegating and of what outside help can contribute to her clients. Patton and Don Corleone, by contrast, are prime examples of individuals who were skilled in using delegation to realize their ends. Effective leaders must delegate and must hone the skill of "guided empowerment." Great leaders understand the abilities of those whom they lead and use that understanding to delegate effectively. Delegation, of course, is more than just giving out assignments; it is having a clear vision of the goals and objectives and challenges facing an organization and then mobilizing the best resources to get the job done. Delegation must be guided, or it can be interpreted as a tactic to shed, not share, responsibility.

Preparation. The quality of good leadership that is most obviously learnable is preparation. While there is more to competence than preparation, there is certainly no competence without preparation. Indeed, it is clear from true-life exploits of Erin Brockovich that preparation is not strictly dependent on education but rather is more closely tied to work ethic and determination, qualities, incidentally, that are also shared by all successful leaders. Just because preparation is something you can learn to do doesn't mean that you should give it short shrift; you still have to work at it. You may get lucky and succeed without preparation on occasion, but dependence on luck in lieu of preparation is a recipe for eventual failure.

Of course, preparation must be done with wisdom or good judgment, and you need to develop a sense for when the time for action has come and additional study may actually threaten the chance for success. Endless preparation without a sense of timing can be as disastrous as being ill-prepared. As Thomas Carlyle once wrote, "The end of man is an action, not a thought." At the same time, we can be sure that action without thought courts failure.

Leaders are in a constant state of preparation. First, leaders prepare to be leaders by honing leadership skills, then they prepare for specific challenges. And as they develop a sense for pinpointing the time to turn the preparation into action, they take that action—and the process begins all over again, as the next challenge is presented.

Focus. Focus is also a skill that can be learned. If you walk through any mall and observe children, you will see a study in the antithesis of focus. What you will observe is frenetic behavior, very limited attention spans and the effect of competing stimuli that can cause a child to be captivated by one thing one minute and something else the next. As we grow up, most of us leave those childish ways behind. Adults are not as easily distracted as children, and their attention spans grow as they mature. Successful leaders have generally learned to deflect distractions and focus on the mission at hand in a laser-like fashion. Some leaders learn to focus through experience, and still others enhance their skill through exercises which sharpen focus. A good example of such exercises is the hand-eye coordination drills used by astronauts and test pilots, and there are exercises designed to develop mental focus as well. Leaders not only have a highly-developed ability to focus but are also able to motivate others to focus.

In every film we've explored, there is an opportunity to observe the quality of focus at work. *Seabiscuit's* title character was probably the most focused of them all, but *Gandhi* and *High Noon* also provide excellent examples. Of course, focus becomes most critical once the mission is defined and a vision is articulated. The mission and the vision are roadmaps of a sort that tell everyone in an organization where the focus should be. Intensity of focus on the right things is a requirement of leadership success.

Negotiation. The skill of negotiating, yet another requirement of a successful leader, is learnable. Humans negotiate all manner of things, and the degree to which leaders hone negotiating skill is the degree to which they invite success. As children, we negotiate with our parents. Beyond childhood, as we gain wisdom and experience, we become more skillful at negotiating. You may recall not getting the answer you wanted from one parent and then making the other parent the target of your negotiating strategy and skill. The usual approach went something like, "Mom didn't mind, but she wanted me to check with you," then to Mom, with "Dad said it was okay." This is not to suggest, of course, that you include deception as part of your negotiating arsenal, but this example shows that even as children we were starting to work on the skills needed to get to "yes." These same skills are valuable and used by all of us in many of life's transactions.

Whether you are trying to get a bigger allowance, wending your way through sticker prices and cash-backs and trade-in values to work out the price of a new car or trying to convince your spouse to allow you go on that extravagant golf trip, you are using negotiating skill. When your mother says you can get a bigger allowance if you clean your room every day, when the salesman says he has to check with his manager, and when your wife says she can consider your golf trip if you will agree that she can go to the spa, they are all negotiating as well. It's not so much about getting what you want, although that may be a part of it, but about putting together "the deal" in a way that everyone can live with, preferably happily.

Great leaders are great negotiators. They have a sense of what is required to achieve the objective. During the negotiations with the Arabs, Golda Meir insisted on meeting her opponents face to face. A journalist suggested that this was not necessary, arguing, "Even divorces are arranged without personal confrontation." "I'm not interested in a divorce," retorted Golda, "I'm interested in a marriage." She had a clear understanding of the objective of the negotiation. Leaders negotiate with colleagues, subordinates, superiors, suppliers, and, often, with competitors, just to name a few. Successful leaders understand what a good result will be in a given instance, and they know what it will take to get that result. One element of negotiating is compromise. Ambrose Bierce defined compromise as "An adjustment of conflicting interests as gives each adversary the satisfaction of thinking he has got what he ought not to have." In today's vernacular, we call it "win-win."

In the course of the negotiation, great leaders know when to compromise and when to hold firm. Gandhi is perhaps the best example, in the films we've examined and elsewhere, of a leader who mastered the art of negotiating. A cursory review of his accomplishments may lead the reviewer to believe that he was uncompromising, but in truth he often compromised to achieve a greater success in the long run. He never compromised his values, and it is vitally important to learn to negotiate effectively without sacrificing principles

While all of the foregoing traits lend themselves to the learning process, there are still other qualities that can be acquired only with the addition of time and experience. These are developed qualities. There are no courses or seminars which certify that these qualities are mastered. They are tested with time and in the field.

Key Leadership Traits That Must Be Practiced

Trust. It has been said that a great leader is trusting and can be trusted. Trust is something I believe you develop over time. It is one of those qualities that we find difficult to define, but we know we look for it in our leaders. All of the leaders we used as models showed us elements of trust. Much has been written about empowerment and delegation as elements of successful leadership, but a leader needs to know to whom tasks and authority should be given. Over time and with experience, we develop that trust. We cannot learn it in books and conferences, and we are not born with it.

Apollo 13 presents a classic example of trust. The highly complex endeavor of launching humans into space requires hundreds of subject-matter experts providing technical input to a flight director who must, in turn, trust that input. The director here developed his trust over time, first by coming to believe in the procedures and the systems that would make up the Apollo 13 mission. With time and experience, he was able to cultivate the trust and have confidence that the trust was justified. Ronald Reagan, when opining on Russian veracity, said, "Trust, but verify." Leaders of complex projects or organizations do not often have the luxury of verification, so they must be able to trust the team and its individual members that make up the team.

Courage. Courage is also a leadership quality that can be developed. Some people believe that courage, which for this discussion can be defined as the absence of fear, is innate, but I am not one of them. Nor do I believe that one can learn courage from lectures, books or classes. Rather, courage—like trust—needs time and experience to develop. Fear of the dentist, fear of certain animals or fear of heights is often overcome with experience and positive exposure. Likewise, individuals who are overcome with fear when they first must make a presentation to a crowd find that their fear diminishes over time as they survive more and more presentations and eventually learn to achieve a certain level of comfort.

Of course, this is not to suggest that there are not legitimate phobias that require professional treatment. But, sometimes, it is just a matter of having the right experiences over time. The courage required by troops as they hit the beach in the face of the enemy, for example, stems from training and repetitive experience. In *Glory*, we observe the ultimate in physical courage that makes the courage required by leaders in other kinds of situations pale by comparison. These are extreme examples of the courage that can be developed, but this illustrates the point that training and repeated exposure to situations that require you to overcome fear can help you to succeed as a leader.

Loyalty. Loyalty is another leadership trait that needs to be developed with the benefit of time and experience. You cannot learn loyalty, in the sense that you can't read a book and find out how it's done. In truth, we are not born loyal to anything but develop loyalty based on our life experiences. Both loyalty and trust are sublimely reflected in an anecdote concerning Einstein's wife, who was once asked if she understood her husband's theory of relativity. "No," she replied, "but I know my husband, and I know he can be trusted." She probably didn't start out having that kind of loyalty and trust in her husband, but her reactions had been borne of her experiences with him over time. Successful leaders are perceived by those whom they lead as being loyal not only to the "cause" but to the team or the troops as well. In *Patton*, we see an intimidating leader who was given to dramatic bombast, brilliant in attacking a coward in order to praise the vast majority of brave soldiers and thus encourage their loyalty. Whether or not you approve of Patton's methods, loyalty to cause and to people is required of leaders, and leaders need to demonstrate their loyalty through actions. Leaders must be loyal to deserve loyalty.

Dedication. Dedication is not a quality that can be learned. Like courage, trust and loyalty, however, dedication is a leadership trait that can be developed. Dedication was one of many leadership qualities touched upon by John F. Kennedy in a 1961 speech to the Massachusetts State Legislature, when he said, "...our success or failure, in whatever office we hold, will be measured by the answers to four questions: First, were we truly men of courage. Second, were we truly men of judgment? Third, were we truly men of integrity? Finally, were we truly men of dedication?" The development of dedication not only requires time and experience, but knowledge and understanding of the cause or the purpose as well. Erin Brockovich is an example of someone who becomes dedicated to her cause after she has her instincts validated by data, anecdotes and hard evidence; the more she learns, the more dedicated she becomes.

Evoking Kennedy once again, it has been amply researched and documented that Kennedy was not dedicated to the cause of Civil Rights during his senatorial tenure or early in his presidency. Over time, his dedication developed through the events of the times and the abject prejudice exhibited by Southern governors. His dedication was demonstrated by the federalization of troops in the South and other acts of political courage. His was a clear case of developed dedication.

Compassion. Compassion is yet another leadership quality that can be developed with the right amount of time and experience. None other than Napoleon I underwent a change of attitude after continuous exposure to the travails of war. He had once, after setting fire to a Russian city and watching the blaze, asked his men if this wasn't a fine sight. When his subordinate replied, "Horrible sire," Napoleon responded by reminding his underling of a Roman emperor's remark, "The corpse of an enemy always smells sweet!" It was some time later that he had a reversal of heart when, along with some of his men, he was reviewing a battlefield as they came across a wounded man crying for help. Napoleon called for a stretcher. "It's only a Russian, sire," said his aide. Napoleon rebuked him by saying, "After a victory, there are no enemies, only men." Time and exposure to the horrors of war had mellowed the great leader and made him more compassionate.

The very definition of compassion—"the deep feeling of sharing the suffering of another, together with the inclination to give aid or show mercy"—identifies it as a quality marked by understanding the pain of another, a quality enhanced by shared experiences. In *12 Angry Men*, the hero shows great compassion for the accused and uses this compassion to persuade the other jurors of a doubt about the man's guilt. We can be sure that this compassion was something developed over the course of the juror's lifetime.

Decisiveness. With decisiveness, we again are faced with a quality of leadership that cannot be learned from any course or conference; but it can be developed and, indeed, *must* be developed by leaders who are to succeed. We have all seen people in leadership positions that are unable to make a decision. In every-day life, this is tolerable. Surely it can be irritating if a companion spends undue time deciding which restaurant to go to or studying the menu after you get there or taking weeks choosing a vacation destination, but this is not life-threatening. It is one thing to be indecisive about recreation; but in business pursuits, a leader needs to be able to judge when he or she has enough data and knowledge to "pull the trigger." Patton had his own take on this notion when he opined, "A good plan violently executed *now* is better than a perfect plan next week."

Without the ability to make timely decisions, a leader can become paralyzed. In some cases, a decision not to decide may be necessary. Chester I. Barnard may have put it best when he wrote, "The fine art of executive decision consists in not deciding questions that are not now pertinent, in not deciding prematurely, in not making decisions that cannot be made effective, and in not making decisions that others should make."

Decisiveness is unnecessary when the answer is obvious or can easily be provided by others. This point was made in Lenny Bruce's rendition of a televangelist's response to a difficult question: "I don't know how much a whole lot of nines are, but I have someone on my staff that knows." Arthur W. Radford suggested that a decision is, "the action an executive must take when he has information so incomplete that the answer does not suggest itself." Decisions must not be made too early, and they cannot be made too late; and it is experience and exposure, "practice," if you will, that allow a leader to make decisions at the appropriate time.

The ability to make decisions is an integral part of being a successful leader. Great leaders have become competent at decision-making not by flying by the seat of their pants or, for that matter, by excruciating data collection. Each experience helps leaders hone this skill and become decisive to the appropriate degree. How much the role of instinct plays is another puzzle of leadership.

You Either Have It or...

There have been many studies on which elements are required for leadership. Recent studies would have us believe that physical height makes a difference. Other studies have shone that gender and race play a role in ascending to leadership positions. This work is not intended to be a scholarly effort that considers such elements but rather a practical, indeed fun, approach to self-improvement dealing in leadership qualities. And the list of qualities culled from the films is not intended to be all-inclusive.

There are many other leadership qualities, some depicted by film characters and some not, which can advance the complex role of a leader. But even if we could come up with a complete list, most effective leaders, even great ones, don't have *all* of those qualities. Still, everyone can aspire to leadership and hone the skills required to practice leadership capably. Are there some qualities we have no chance of honing because these are ones that the great leaders are simply born with?

Innate Qualities. Some qualities do not lend themselves to learning or developing. Most talented people like to believe that they can be leaders and can even point to instances in which they have served in a leadership role. But occasional instances of leadership do not a leader make. Complex projects, large organizations and long term strategies generally require sustained exceptional leadership, and not everyone is suited to that task. Some people will never be suited to leadership, and still others will only achieve a modicum of leadership success. If you desire to improve as a leader, there are a variety of avenues to pursue toward that end.

We've talked about how you can enhance yourself as a leader by building your bank of leadership qualities, particularly by learning or developing those in which you are not strong. Still, it is true that some qualities exhibited by the most accomplished leaders are innate. These qualities are natural, some might even say inborn, an integral part of some individuals' make-up. These qualities may even separate the great leader from the good leader. Among the film characters that were explored, probably only Gandhi and Patton could claim the distinction of being called great leaders. These men had qualities that were learned and developed over time, but they also possessed qualities that superseded normal traits. Those are the "gifted" qualities. While I believe that you either have these qualities or don't, it is worth studying them and identifying what you might do if you were not graced with those inherent qualities—charisma, passion and vision.

Charisma. Max Weber, when writing "Economy and Society" in 1922, wrote, "Charisma knows only inner determination and inner restraint. The charismatic leader gains and maintains authority solely by proving his strength in life." Charisma is defined by *The American Heritage Dictionary* as "a. A rare quality or power attributed to those persons who have demonstrated an exceptional ability for winning the devotion of large numbers of people. b. A special quality of personal magnetism or charm." Few readers of this text would describe themselves as charismatic, but many are very good leaders nonetheless. The charismatic leader is the one lay folk are talking about when they say, "He lights up the room when he walks in," or "She draws people to her like honey draws bees." I believe charisma is a quality that those fortunate enough to possess it, and hopefully to use it to good ends, have come by naturally. But leaders can develop some of the attributes of charisma with much the same effect. Examples of charismatic attributes would include things like a positive demeanor, taking a keen interest in others and listening to what they say, active curiosity and optimism. Working on these kinds of characteristics may not make you charismatic, but I believe that it can help you approach the magnetism of someone who is thought of as charismatic. You may not become a Gandhi or a Patton, but you can come closer to the lofty places they occupy in the annals of leaders.

Passion. Among the innate qualities, there is also passion, which *The American Heritage Dictionary* tells us is "A powerful emotion or appetite" or "boundless enthusiasm." Lytton Strachey, an English writer of the early 1900's, when asked what he considered the greatest thing in life, responded without hesitation, "Why, passion, of course." It is no doubt true that each of us is passionate about something, but being a passionate person is more than that; it is having a certain emotional fervor and zest for life that transcends everything else. Any description of Patton would fall short unless it included the recognition of his passion. Although possessed of a quieter passion, Gandhi was also a man who was propelled by his passion.

Whenever a great leader is observed leading his or her forces, whenever that leader describes the challenge or talks about the work, even when that person is at play, there is a certain passion that permeates every word and every action. Oliver Wendell Holmes, Jr. described it eloquently, when he said, "Life is action and passion; therefore, it is required of a man that he should share the passion and action of the time, at peril of being judged not to have lived." Great leaders are passionate about every aspect of life. If you don't have passion, you can still be a good leader by being more animated, by presenting a forceful demeanor and by more directly engaging others through eye contact and, allowing for gender sensitivity, physical contact.

While you may not be able to acquire passion, you can exude a more passionate countenance. It has already been fairly said that everyone is passionate about something, so the passion gene is within us, but few are blessed to be able to express it naturally.

Vision. Our friends at *The American Heritage Dictionary* provide us with several definitions of vision which include "unusual competence in discernment or perception; intelligent foresight" and "a mental image produced by the imagination." Not unlike charisma and passion, vision does not lend itself to pragmatic definition. Nor does it lend itself to acquisition.

Great leaders display an ability to "see" the end before the project or challenge even begins. They often have a sense of how events will play out before those events get underway. Gandhi envisioned the exit of the British from India far before even the first victory was achieved. Patton had remarkable instincts about upcoming battles, which he explained by claiming a prior life. The Godfather "knew" that it was not the Tattaglia brothers, but instead Barzini, that was responsible for treachery. Perhaps it was put best by Jonathan Swift in *Thoughts on Various Subjects* in 1711: "Vision is the art of seeing things invisible." Whether you call it vision or instinct or intuition, it is a characteristic that some seem to come by naturally. If you are not one of those with the gift of vision, you have it in your power to learn the art of observing and analyzing what is going on around you, what might hurt you and what might help you, and anticipating what might lie ahead.

So, great leaders have been blessed with certain innate qualities, charisma, passion and vision most notably among them, but the rest of us need not despair. Good leaders can enhance their competence by understanding the nature of these innate traits and emulating discrete elements of them. If you were not born with these traits you may never become a leader that is written about in the history books. You may never have bridges or highways named after you, and you may never be remembered for a specific victory. But you can certainly become a formidable leader with extraordinary success. You can be counted among those who are named when people are asked "Who had the greatest influence in your career?" Continuous attention to, and improvement in, all leadership areas is, in the end, the key to success.

# 15 COMING ATTRACTIONS

Maximizing You

The coming attraction is you—the new you that is based on learning, honing and practicing the qualities of leadership. You needn't read a plethora of self-help books or attend seminars or conferences that promise to reveal leadership secrets. To be sure, those exercises could enhance and accelerate your understanding of leadership skills, but there is much you can do on your own to augment your leadership talent.

You are invited to peruse the films offered in this book with a view toward observing and understanding leadership qualities. There are many nuances of leadership in those films that were not explored in this text but which are worthy of observation and analysis nonetheless. Further, there are literally hundreds of other films which set forth excellent examples of leadership qualities. Part of my intent here is to encourage the readers to view films through a different lens, with the hope that you will be prompted to seek out and study the various qualities that many characters portray. There is a rich mine of material in films of every genre.

Even the most mundane films, those with perhaps a less than intellectual bent, can offer leadership lessons. *Animal House* is a good example of a farce which lends support to this assertion. Toward the end of the film, the lead character, Bluto, played by the late John Belushi, tries to inspire his fellow brothers in his flawed fraternity to follow him as he plans to vent his outrage by wreaking havoc on the coming community parade. With great verve, he gives a dramatic plea that gets the complete attention of the gathered group. At the conclusion of his entreaty, he rises up, and, in a great burst of energy and amidst a crescendo of shouts, he exhorts the group to join him and take up his cause. With a great bellow, his fist raised in the air, he runs out of the room, fully expecting a stampede of followers. The camera remains focused on the room, where the brothers' lack of movement and complete apathy make them look like statues. Like Will Kane in *High Noon*, Bluto failed to inspire. The failure to inspire happened in a different way but with the same result, and this is but one example of how the same leadership quality or shortcoming can be aptly portrayed in very different ways with different characters in different settings. You should enjoy the search for these and other examples.

Observation Is a Teacher

Outside of the world of film, there are events in everyday life that offer leadership insight. We observe acts of leadership each day, as in the example mentioned earlier of the selfless good citizen who directs other vehicles around a traffic jam. If, by reading this book, you have been enticed to look at leadership qualities in a new light, then you will hopefully carry your new perspective with you into your personal as well as your professional life. In life, as in film, there are acts of leadership large and small, and, by emulating these acts in your own milieu, you can greatly enhance your leadership skills.

What does one do with this new knowledge and perspective on leadership qualities? Each of us is challenged to improve ourselves. Many of us have been judged by others through formal job evaluations or the informal assessments of friends and colleagues. When others judge us, they often compare us against the qualities explored in this work as they try to determine whether or not and to what degree we exhibit integrity, courage, preparation, respect and other qualities. Those who would judge us include our boss, colleagues, friends, acquaintances and family members who have come to know us in a variety of contexts. They do, in fact, know us, some more than others, but there is only one person who can rightly claim to know the total person in all of his or her contexts. That one person is the one that each of us sees in the mirror.

When we look at ourselves, we can see a picture that includes all of our qualities and all of our faults. Even more than our closest confidante or spouse, that person reflected in the mirror knows the best and the worst in us. With that complete and intimate knowledge, everyone can set a course to improve. Self-improvement can come in many ways, but in the case of leadership quality enhancement, you can try to adopt the positive qualities studied in the movies looked at here and abandon the traits that detract from those qualities. You can, for example, train yourself to "count to ten" when road rage threatens to erupt, and you can reach deep down to call upon core values when apathy or temptation beckons. In the final analysis, only you can effect fundamental change in your own makeup.

In our increasingly fast-paced lives, we are often given the opportunity to assess our traits as events thrust us into new environments on a regular basis. The days of an individual being with one company for an entire career are evaporating at a dizzying pace. The reasons are varied, but the fact is inexorable. It is relatively rare when a company survives for thirty years without change in today's world of mergers, acquisitions, bankruptcies, divestitures and globalization, so it should not surprise us that most professionals entering the work force today may work for several different companies in their career lifetimes. Even during the time we spend in one organization, we are likely to change assignments, get promoted, get transferred or be given a new set of mission statements to adhere to. These are all fantastic opportunities.

Every major or even minor change in the workplace provides an occasion to make personal change. In the case of any change which offers you a new set of players with whom you will be interacting, you are afforded the chance to make a significant change in yourself, to "re-invent" yourself, if you will. Take the case of a promotion to a leadership position requiring a geographical move. Chances are that most, if not all, of those with whom you will be working will not yet "know" you. Be assured that your new co-workers will not miss the occasion to judge you on your first few encounters. What a wonderful opportunity this affords you to try and roll out the good and strip away the bad in terms of the kind of leader that you want to be. Even with more modest changes in circumstances, you can make modest improvements. Look at every change in assignment or working conditions as a chance to be—and be known as—a better person. This, of course, has implications for your life outside of the workplace as well.

It seems axiomatic that the qualities of leadership discussed in the films and the additional ones mentioned in the forthcoming Short Subjects are qualities to be admired. To the degree that you can incorporate these qualities into your own approach, you can become a fuller, more effective leader. As you study these qualities in the special context of the films, give some thought to how they might fit into your own life experiences. If your acuity concerning the qualities, traits and characteristics of leaders has been enhanced and your desire and ability to improve your own leadership approach has been stimulated, then the purpose for this book has been fulfilled. You will become a better leader, something you owe to yourself, to those above and below you on the corporate ladder and those with whom you share your life.

Remember, leadership sets the tone for any organization, for a family of four or a Fortune 100 Company with global reach. Best-selling author and economist Steven D. Levitt, Ph.D., interpreting from a recent government study of 20,000 American children from kindergarten through fifth grade, wrote in the October 2005 issue of *Bottom Line* that, "What really sparks a child's intelligence is not the act of being read to, but living in an environment where books, learning and achievement are prized." That conclusion supports the premise that leadership, by parents or by anyone else seeking to lead, can set the stage for success. What tone will you set in your family, your workplace or your social life? Observing the traits of leaders as portrayed on film and setting out to embrace those qualities in your own leadership roles will improve and enrich your performance at work and in life.

The United States Army says, "Be all you can be." I say, "Maximize your talents."

16 SHORT SUBJECTS

The Films

E ach of the films in this book was selected for a specific quality or trait that is displayed by one or more of the characters. In most cases, films were chosen because particular scenes best depict, and particular characters best personify, the leadership trait to be examined. All of the films are worthy of a full viewing, and the observant viewer will often find that a review of certain key scenes can further your understanding of the quality that was analyzed here, as well as other qualities that you can identify and examine on your own. The intent is to pique the interest of the student, the practitioner of leadership, if you will, who will hopefully be inspired to study the various qualities featured in this book in the complete context of the films. The full flavor can only be savored when you are able to see the expressions and body language and consider what is happening in light of what comes before and after.

To assist you in your further cinematic review, what follows is additional information concerning each film. I have provided some cogent quotes which are emblematic of additional leadership qualities. I hope you will enjoy locating the scenes that are referenced and go on to apply your own perspective to each film as you find these and other qualities. For your further enjoyment and leadership development, I have referenced some other films of a similar genre that may offer lessons of their own.

Lawrence of Arabia

Directed by: David Lean

Released in: 1962

Length: 216 minutes

Highlighted leadership quality: Adaptability

The Cast

T.E. Lawrence - Peter O'Toole

Prince Feisal - Alec Guinness

Auda abu Tayi - Anthony Quinn

General Lord Edmund Allenby - Jack Hawkins

Sherif Ali - Omar Sharif

Turkish Bey - José Ferrer

Colonel Brighton - Anthony Quayle

Mr. Dryden - Claude Rains

Jackson Bentley - Arthur Kennedy

General Sir Archibald Murray - Donald Wolfit

Gasim - I.S. Johar

Majid - Gamil Ratib

Farraj - Michel Ray

Daud - John Dimech

Tafas - Zia Mohyeddin

Additional leadership qualities depicted in *Lawrence of Arabia*

Ability to inspire. "My friends we have been foolish, Auda will not come to Aqaba. Not for money and not for Feisal, and not to drive away the Turks...No he will come because it is his pleasure."

Confidence. "The best of them won't come for money; they'll come for me."

Creativity. "A thousand Arabs means a thousand knives, delivered anywhere day or night. It means a thousand camels. That means a thousand packs of high explosives and a thousand crack rifles. We can cross Arabia while Johnny Turk is still turning round, and smash his railways. And while he's mending them, I'll smash them somewhere else. In thirteen weeks, I can have Arabia in chaos."

Resoluteness. "My lord, I think your book is right. The desert is an ocean in which no oar is dipped and on this ocean the Bedu go where they please and strike where they please. This is the way the Bedu have always fought. You're famed throughout the world for fighting in this way and this is the way you should fight now!"

Compassion. "We took them prisoners; the entire garrison. No, that's not true. We killed some; too many really. I'll manage it better next time."

Boldness. After marching into a bar with a dirty Bedouin he is told to leave because it is for British officers! Lawrence replies boldly, "That's alright. We're not particular."

Vision. "So long as the Arabs fight tribe against tribe, so long will they be a little people, a silly people-greedy, barbarous, and cruel."

Other films having similar themes or lessons
Bridge Over the River Kwai (1957)

The Last Samurai (2003)

The Four Feathers (2003)

Gandhi

Directed by: Richard Attenborough
Released in: 1982
Length: 188 minutes

Highlighted leadership quality: Respect

The Cast

Mohandas K. Gandhi - Ben Kinglsey
Margaret Bourke-White - Candice Bergen
Gen. Reginald Dyer - Edward Fox
Lord Irwin - John Gielgud
Judge Broomfield - Trevor Howard
Lord Chelmsford - John Mills
Vince Walker - Martin Sheen
Rev. Charlie Andrews - Ian Charleson
Pandit Nehru - Roshan Seth
General Smuts - Athol Fugard
Kasturbsa Gandhi - Rohini Kattangadi
Kahn - Amrish Puri
Sandar Patel - Saeed Jaffrey

Additional leadership qualities depicted
in *Gandhi*

Courage. "You may torture my body, break my bones, even kill me, then they will have my dead body. Not my obedience."

Resoluteness. "The function of a civil resistance is to provoke response and we will provoke until they respond or change the law. They are not in control; we are."

Vision. "Whenever I despair, I remember that the way of truth and love has always won. There may be tyrants and murderers, and for a time, they may seem invincible, but in the end, they always fail. Think of it: always."

Insight. "I beg you to accept that there is no people on Earth who would not prefer their own bad government to the good government of an alien power."

Decisiveness. "We think it is time that you recognize that you are masters in someone else's home. Despite the best intentions of the best of you, you must, in the nature of things, humiliate us to control us. It is time you left."

Ability to inspire. "I am a Muslim and a Hindu and a Christian and a Jew and so are all of you."

Other films having similar themes or lessons

Passage to India (1982)
The Last Emperor (1987)
Malcolm X (1992)

The Godfather

Directed by: Mario Puzo
Released in: 1972
Length: 175 minutes

Highlighted leadership quality: Self-Control

The Cast

Don Vito Corleone - Marlon Brando
Michael Corleone - Al Pacino
Santino Corleone - James Caan
Pete Clemenza - Richard S. Castellano
Tom Hagen - Robert Duvall
Captain McCluskey - Sterling Hayden
Jack Woltz - John Marley
Emilio Barzini - Richard Conte
Virgil Sollozzo - Al Lettieri
Kay Adams - Diane Keaton
Salvadore Tessio - Abe Vigoda
Connie - Talia Shire
Carlo Rizzi - Gianni Russo
Fredo - John Cazale

Additional leadership qualities depicted
in *The Godfather*

Core value strength. "Do you spend time with your family? Good. Because a man that doesn't spend time with his family can never be a real man."

Insight. "Tattaglia's a pimp. He never could've outfought Santino. But I didn't know until this day that it was Barzini all along."

Strategic skill. "Never let anyone outside the family know what you're thinking."

Compassion. "If you'd come to me in friendship, then this scum that ruined your daughter would be suffering this very day. And if by chance an honest man like yourself should make enemies, than they would become my enemies."

Confidence. "I'll make him an offer he can't refuse."

Clarity. "I'm a superstitious man, and if some unlucky accident should befall Michael—if he is to be shot in the head by a police officer, or be found hung dead in a jail cell...or if he should be struck by a bolt of lightning—then I'm going to blame some of the people in this room; and then I do not forgive."

Other films having similar themes or lessons

Once Upon a Time in America (1984)

The Godfather Trilogy: 1901 - 1980 (1992)

Goodfellas (1990)

Apollo 13 (1995)

The Right Stuff (1983)

Bugsy (1991)

Apollo 13

Directed by: Ron Howard
Released in: 1995
Length: 140 minutes

Highlighted leadership trait: Innovativeness

The Cast

Jim Lovell - Tom Hanks

Fred Haise - Bill Paxton

Jack Swigert - Kevin Bacon

Ken Mattingly - Gary Sinise

Gene Kranz - Ed Harris

Marilyn Lovell - Kathleen Quinlan

Barbara Lovell - Mary Kate Schellhardt

Susan Lovell - Emily Ann Lloyd

Jeffrey Lovell - Miko Hughes

Mary Haise - Tracy Reiner

Deke Slayton - Chris Ellis

Blanch Lovel - Jean Howard

Pete Conrad - David Andrews

Additional leadership qualities depicted
in *Apollo 13*

Compassion. "Just a little while longer Freddo. Just a little while longer, we're gonna hit that water in the South Pacific. Open up that hatch. It's 80 degrees out there."

Confidence. "With all due respect, sir, I believe this is gonna be our finest hour."

Resoluteness. "We've never lost an American in space, we're sure as hell not gonna lose one on my watch! Failure is not an option."

Self-control. "Let's work the problem people. Let's not make things worse by guessing."

Vision. "I sometimes catch myself looking up at the moon, remembering the changes of fortune in our long voyage, thinking of the thousands of people who worked to bring the three of us home. I look up at the moon, and wonder: When will we be going back? And who will that be?"

Boldness. "I don't care about what anything was designed to do, I care about what it can do."

Ability to inspire. "Gentleman, it's been a privilege flying with you."

Other films having similar themes or lessons

The Right Stuff (1983)

Mission to Mars (2000)

Erin Brockovich

Directed by: Steven Soderbergh

Released in: 2000

Length: 130 minutes

Highlighted leadership quality: Preparation

The Cast

Erin Brockovich - Julia Roberts

Dr. Jaffe - David Brisbin

Rosalind - Dawn Didawick

Ed Masry - Albert Finney

Donald - Valente Rodriguez

Brenda - Conchata Ferrell

Los Angeles Judge - George Rocky Sullivan

Defending Lawyer - Pat Skipper

Defendant - Jack Gill

Mrs. Morales - Irene Olga Lopez

Julia (Waitress) - Erin Brockovich-Ellis

Matthew - Scotty Leavenworth

Katie - Gemmenne de la Pena

Additional leadership qualities depicted
in *Erin Brockovich*

Honesty. "For the first time in my life, I got people respecting me. Please, don't ask me to give it up."

Confidence. "Well as long as I have one ass instead of two I'll wear what I like if that's all right with you? You might want to re-think those ties."

Passion. "Not personal! That is my work, my sweat, and my time away from my kids! If that is not personal, I don't know what is!"

Ability to inspire. "Second of all, these people don't dream about being rich. They dream about being able to watch their kids swim in a pool without worrying that they'll have to have a hysterectomy at the age of twenty, like Rosa Diaz, a client of ours. Or having their spine deteriorate, like Stan Blume, another client of ours. So before you come back here with another lame ass offer, I want you to think real hard about what your spine is worth Mr. Walker. Or what you might expect someone to pay you for your uterus Ms. Sanchez."

Insight. "Bullshit. If you had a full staff, this office would return a client's damn phone calls."

Other films having similar themes or lessons

A Civil Action (1998)

The China Syndrome (1979)

Silkwood (1983)

No Way Out (1987)

JFK (1981)

High Noon

Directed by: Fred Zinnemann

Released in: 1952

Length: 85 minutes

Highlighted leadership quality: Ability to inspire

The Cast

Marshall Will Kane - Gary Cooper

Mayor Jonas Henderson - Thomas Mitchell

Deputy Sheriff Harvey Pell - Lloyd Bridges

Helen Ramirez - Katy Jurado

Amy Fowler Kane - Grace Kelly

Judge Percy Mettrick - Otto Kruger

Martin Howe - Lon Chaney, Jr.

Sam Fuller - Harry Morgan

Frank Miller - Ian MacDonald

Mildred Fuller - Eve McVeagh

Minister Mahin - Morgan Farley

Cooper - Harry Shannon

Jack Colby - Lee Van Cleef

Ben Miller - Sheb Wooley

Additional leadership qualities depicted
in *High Noon*

Core value strength. "I've heard guns. My father and my brother were killed by guns. They were on the right side but that didn't help them any when the shooting started. My brother was nineteen. I watched him die. That's when I became a Quaker. I don't care who's right or who's wrong. There's got to be some better way for people to live."

Passion. "I don't understand you. No matter what you say. If Kane was my man, I'd never leave him like this. I'd get a gun. I'd fight."

Compassion. "You risk your skin catching killers and the juries turn them loose so they can come back and shoot at you again. If you're honest you're poor your whole life and in the end you wind up dying all alone on some dirty street. For what? For nothing. For a tin star."

Resoluteness. "Don't shove me Harv. I'm tired of being shoved."

Other films having similar themes or lessons

Rio Bravo (1959)

High Plains Drifter (1973)

The Shootist (1973)

The Magnificent Seven (1960)

The Ox-Bow Incident (1943)

12 Angry Men

Directed by: Sidney Lumet

Released in: 1957

Length: 96 minutes

Highlighted leadership quality: Judgment

The Cast

Juror #1 - Martin Balsam

Juror #2 - John Fiedler

Juror #3 - Lee J. Cobb

Juror #4 - E.G. Marshall

Juror #5 - Jack Klugman

Juror #6 - Ed Binns

Juror #7 - Jack Warden

Juror #8 - Henry Fonda

Juror #9 - Joseph Sweeney

Juror #10 - Ed Begley

Juror #11 - George Voskoves

Juror #12 - Robert Webber

Additional leadership qualities depicted in *12 Angry Men*

Rationality. "But supposing he really did hear it. This phrase, how many times has each of us used it? Probably hundreds." "I could kill you for that, darling." "If you do that once more, junior, I'm going to kill you." "But supposing..."

Passion. "Well, say something! You lousy bunch of bleedin' hearts. You're not goin' to intimidate me! I'm entitled to my own opinion!"

Resoluteness. "Nobody has to prove otherwise. The burden of proof is on the prosecution. The defendant doesn't even have to open his mouth. That's in the Constitution."

Probing nature. "I don't feel I have to be loyal to one side or the other. I'm just asking questions."

Core value strength. "For the same reason you are not: it's the way I was brought up."

Other films having similar themes or lessons

Runaway Jury (2003)
To Kill a Mockingbird (1962)
The Ox-Bow Incident (1943)

One Flew Over the Cuckoo's Nest

Directed by: Milos Forman
Released in: 1975
Length: 133 minutes

Highlighted leadership quality: Focus

The Cast

Randle Patrick McMurphy - Jack Nicholson
Nurse Mildred Ratched - Louise Fletcher
Harding - William Redfield
Ellis - Michael Berryman
Colonel Matterson - Peter Brocco
Dr. John Sopivey - Dean R. Brooks
Miller - Alonzo Brown
Orderly Turkle - Scatman Crothers
Attendant Warren - Mwako Cumbuka
Martini - Danny Devito
William Duell - Jim Sefelt
Bancini - Josip Elic
Nurse Itsu - Lan Fendors
Attendant Washington - Nathan George

Additional leadership qualities depicted in *One Flew Over the Cuckoo's Nest*

Confidence. "I'm a goddamn marvel of modern science."

Compassion. "What do you think you are, for Chrissake, crazy or somethin'? Well you're not! You're no crazier than the average asshole out walkin' around on the streets and that's it."

Commitment. "I'm not goin' without you, Mac. I wouldn't leave you this way...You're coming with me."

Creativity. "Koufax looks down! He's looking at the great Mickey Mantle now! Here comes the pitch! Mantle swings! It's a f***ing home run!"

Other films having similar themes or lessons

Forest Gump (1994)

Midnight Cowboy (1969)

Girl Interrupted (1999)

The Deer Hunter (1978)

The Snake Pit (1948)

The Three Faces of Eve (1957)

The Prince of Tides (1991)

Glory

Directed by: Edward Zwick
Released in: 1989
Length: 122 minutes

Highlighted leadership quality: Courage

The Cast

Colonel Robert Gould Shaw - Matthew Broderick
Private Trip - Denzel Washington
Major Cabot Forbes - Cary Elwes
Sgt. Major John Rowlins - Morgan Freeman
Private Jupiter Sharts - Jihmi Kennedy
Corporal Thomas Searles - Andre Braugher
Sgt. Major Muleahy - John Finn
Captain Charles Fessenden Morse - Donovan Leitch
Henry Sturgis Russell - J.D. Cullum
Governor John Albion Andrew - Alan North
General Harker - Bob Gunton
Colonel James M. Montgomery - Cliff De Young
Christian Baskous - Edward L. Pierce
General George Strong - Jay O. Sanders

Additional leadership qualities depicted
in *Glory*

Ability to inspire. "And who are you? So full of hate that you have to fight everybody, because you've been whipped and chased by hounds. Well that might not be living, but it sure as hell ain't dying. And dying's been what these white boys have been doing for going on three years now, dying by the thousands, dying for you fool."

Core value strength. "Let me fight with the rifle in one hand, and the Good Book in the other. So that if I may die at the muzzle of the rifle... die on water, or on land, I may know that you blessed Jesus almighty are with me... and I have no fear."

Confidence. "There wouldn't be nothing but rebs dyin' if they'd let the fifty-fourth in it."

Compassion. "I have no doubt that you are a fair man, Mulcahy. I wonder if you are treating the men a little hard."

Dedication. "Y'all's the onliest family I got. I love the 54th. Ain't even much a matter what happens tomorrow, 'cause we men, ain't we?"

Other films having similar themes or lessons
Black Hawk Down (2001)
We Were Soldiers (2002)
The Patriot (2000)

The Contender

Directed by: Rod Lurie
Released in: 2000
Length: 126 minutes

Highlighted leadership quality: Integrity

The Cast

Representative Sheldon Runyon - Gay Oldman
Senator Laine Hanson - Joan Allen
President Jackson Evans - Jeff Bridges
Representative Reginald Webster - Christian Slater
Kermit Newman - Sam Elliott
Governor Jack Hathaway - William L. Petersen
Jerry Tolliver - Saul Rubinek
Oscar Billings - Philip Baker Hall
William Hanson - Robin Thomas
Cynthia Charlton Lee - Mariel Hemingway
Agent Paige Willomina - Kathryn Morris
Fiona Hathaway - Kristen Shaw
Makerowitz - Douglas Urbanski
Timmy - Noah Fryrear

Additional leadership qualities depicted
in *The Contender*

Core value strength. "Come on, Kermit. If we do that, we are no better than he is."

Ability to inspire. "Napoleon once said when asked to explain the lack of great statesmen in the world, that 'to get power you need to display absolute pettiness; to exercise power, you need to show true greatness.' Such pettiness and greatness are rarely found in one person... Laine Hanson has asked that I allow her to step aside. She asked me to do this because she wants my presidency to end on a note of triumph and not controversy. Understand those of you who worked to bring her down, that she asked to have her name withdrawn from consideration, not because she isn't great, but because she isn't petty. Because those two forms of leadership traits could not live in her body or her soul. Greatness. It comes in many forms, sometimes it comes in the form of sacrifice—that's the loneliest form."

Confidence. "What I say the American people will believe. And do you know why? Because I will have a very big microphone in front of me."

Boldness. "Greatness is the orphan of urgency, Laine. Greatness only emerges when we need it most... in time of war or calamity. I can't ask somebody to be a Kennedy or a Lincoln. What I can ask for is the promise of greatness. And that, Madam Senator...you don't have."

Other films having similar themes or lessons

All the Kings Men (1949)

Advise & Consent (1962)

Enemy of the State (1998)

Primary Colors (1998)

Arlington Road (1999)

The Sum of All Fears (2002)

All the Presidents Men (1976)

Patton

Directed by: Franklin J. Schaffner
Released in: 1970
Length: 170 minutes

Highlighted leadership quality: Core value strength

The Cast

General George S. Patton - George C. Scott
General Omar N. Bradley - Karl Malden
Captain Chester B. Hansen - Stephen Young
Brig. General Hobart Carver - Michael Strong
General Bradley's Driver - Carey Loftin
Moroccan Minister - Albert Dumotier
Lt. Colonel Henry Davenport - Frank Latimore
Captain Richard N. Jenson - Morgan Paull
Field Marchal Erwin Rommel - Karl Michael Vogler
General Patton's Driver - Bill Hickman
Colonel Gaston Bell - Lawrence Dobkin
Air Marshall Coningham - John Barrie
Lt. General Buford - David Bauer
Lt. Colonel Codman - Paul Stevens

Additional leadership qualities depicted in *Patton*

Vision. "The Carthaginians defending the city were attacked by three Roman legions. They were proud and brave but they couldn't hold. They were massacred. Arab women stripped them of their tunics and their swords and lances. The soldiers lay naked in the sun. Two thousand years ago. I was here."

Ability to inspire. "Men, all this stuff you've heard about America not wanting to fight—wanting to stay out of the war, is a lot of horse dung, Americans traditionally love to fight. All real Americans love the sting of battle. When you were kids, you all admired the champion marble shooter, the fastest runner, big league ball players, the toughest boxers. Americans love a winner and will not tolerate a loser. Americans play to win all the time. I wouldn't give a hoot in hell for a man who lost and laughed. That's why Americans have never lost and never will lose a war, because the very thought of losing is hateful to Americans."

Courage. "We're gonna keep fighting. Is that clear? We're gonna attack all night, we're gonna attack the next morning. If we're not victorious, let no man come back alive."

Insight. "There's one big difference between you and me, George. I do this job because I've been trained to do it. You do it because you love it."

Confidence. "In ten days I'll have a war on with those Communist bastards, and I'll make it look like their fault."

Boldness. "We're not just going to shoot the bastards, were going to cut out their living guts and use them to grease the treads on our tanks."

Other films having similar themes or lessons

The Longest Day (1962)

Saving Private Ryan (1998)

The Big Red One (1960)

Seabiscuit

Directed by: Gary Ross
Released in: 2003
Length: 141 minutes

Highlighted leadership quality: Determination

The Cast

Narrator - David McCullough
Charles Howard - Jeff Bridges
Tom Smith - Chris Cooper
Red Pollard - Tobey Maguire
Tick Tock McGlaughlin - William Macy
Marcela Howard - Elizabeth Banks
Annie Howard - Calerie Mahaffey
Mr. Pollard - Michael O'Neill
Mrs. Pollard - Annie Corley
Landbroker - David Doty
Steamer Owner - Michael Ensign
Sam - Carl Craig
Car Customer - James Keane

Additional leadership qualities depicted
in *Seabiscuit*

Compassion. "I think it's better to break a man's leg than his heart."

Insight. "You know, everybody thinks we found this broken-down horse and fixed him. But we didn't. He fixed us; every one of us. And I guess in a way, we kinda fixed each other too."

Confidence. "It wouldn't be fair to us. It wouldn't be fair to them either. You wouldn't put Jack Dempsey in the ring with a middle-weight would you?"

Optimism. "He just said it's possible. Well, hell, anything's possible. We've proved that already."

Other films having similar themes or lessons
The Legend of Bagger Vance (2002)
The Rocky Series (1976-1990)
The Story of Seabiscuit (1949)
Seabiscuit the Lost Documentary (1939)
Black Beauty (1994)
Cinderella Man (2005)

# EPILOGUE

Afterthoughts

"Epilogue. A speech addressed to an
audience at the end of a play." ...Webster

This is the end of a play of sorts. As you may have gathered, I am much better at communicating through the
spoken word than through the written. That said, I
hope that you will stick with me as I pretend that you are here,
and I will share with you some general thoughts about this
book and some random thoughts on leaders and leadership.

The Films

There were times during the process of writing this book
that I questioned my selection of movies. I had the usual concerns
about political correctness: I felt that I needed something about a
woman, something about people of color, something that would
appeal to various audiences—the Gen-X population, yuppies, yip-
pies, contemporary leaders and so on. But then I concluded that
the book should be less about the movies and more about the
leadership qualities to be showcased, so I used that as the primary
basis for selection.

I also wanted to include what I think of as entertaining
flicks that you would be encouraged to buy or borrow or rent to do
your own analysis of the leadership traits that they depict.

And, lastly, I wanted to ensure that the selected films were ones in which the character exhibits the body language and facial expressions that confirm my point about the value of observing the leadership process in full context.

I suppose it goes without saying that I am satisfied with the result. I would appreciate hearing your views on other films that might be explored to further this study of leadership. Drop me a note at publishpaladin@aol.com, and let me hear what you think. I promise to consider all of your ideas if I ever get around to writing a sequel.

Fiction or Fact

Another thought occurred to me during this effort having to do with the real-life characters that formed the basis for the characters in some of the films. I attempted to deal with these people and their backgrounds as they were depicted in the film treatments, mindful of the fact that the film renditions were occasionally at odds in one way or another with the true-to-life details. In the movie version of *Seabiscuit*, for example, some facts were omitted, presumably for dramatic effect. An illustration of this is that Charles Howard and his friend Bing Crosby invested in the construction of Santa Anita race track and made a good deal of money on the track, as well as on automobiles.

I opted for the practical approach by simply taking the "facts" as presented on the screen and attempting to make my leadership points based less on absolute historical truth and more on what the various scenes portrayed.

The Audience

I have, of necessity, made certain assumptions regarding the people who read books of this ilk. Perhaps the biggest assumption is that the majority of the readers will be people who want to improve themselves in the workplace and in their personal lives.

In structuring these lessons from the big screen, I was also impacted by my belief, one that was at the very foundation of *Reel Lessons*, that people, in the workplace in particular, fall into three separate categories—underachievers, overachievers and maximizers. Yet, as I have observed successful people in the workplace, I have noticed that while particular qualities seem to be more pronounced in one category or another, there are some qualities that are common to all leaders, at least successful ones; these universal categories are ambition, hard work and the willingness to take some degree of risk.

In some ways, it is all about expectations. We all know the expression "She is not living up to her potential." Parents say it, teachers say it, and supervisors say it. Perhaps the point can best be made by taking another look at some of the movie characters in these three categories I've mentioned: overachievers, underachievers and maximizers.

Three Categories

Overachievers. Erin Brockovich is a fine example of an overachiever. Her level of success went far beyond what might have been predicted given her limited formal education and means. She exceeded all expectations, perhaps even her own, by defying conventional wisdom, squeezing every drop of potential out of every opportunity, using creativity in problem solving. She was tenacious, not easily discouraged, and she took calculated risks.

The success of the overachiever who goes well beyond what anyone might expect is often attributed to luck. In some cases, there may some element of truth to that, but the more important distinction of the overachiever is the determination to make the most out of circumstance and ability, despite whatever limitations might exist. As I write this, I think of Jesse V., Dean D. and myself as possibly fitting into this category. As you read this, what names come to your mind?

Underachievers. Although he had to overcome a lot to take on any leadership role at all, R.P. McMurphy is an underachiever. He appears to have some education, he is articulate, and his charm borders on charisma. He can be witty, inspiring, sometimes befriended by rationality and logic. He is even, at times, creative as he moves to execute some plan. And yet, he never achieves his potential. Often his own worst enemy, he frequently finds a way to lose. Joe V. comes to my mind for this category.

The relative lack of success of underachievers, those who don't go as far as their circumstances, talent or expectations suggest that they should, is often attributed to bad breaks. Again, there may be something to that in some cases, but it's really more than that. While underachievers are not all looking for a way to lose, they are all individuals who are able to tolerate not making the most of their careers. Carol D. comes to my mind as a self-described underachiever whose talent far exceeds her ambition. Can you name and describe an underachiever?

Maximizers. Patton, looking for every way conceivable way to achieve and bolster his success, was a maximizer, if ever there was one. He was formally educated in elite schools, he thrived on competition, and he was diligent in studying his craft. As he went through all the necessary hoops for advancement, he was dedicated, he was passionate, and he was indefatigable in his quest for success.

The success of a maximizer can appear to be effortless—but is not. Maximizers exert every possible effort and avail themselves of every possible opportunity for success. Whether or not they exceed expectations, they leave nothing to chance. My friend Phillip L., a classic in this category, immediately comes to mind. Name and describe someone you know who meets the definition.

Achievement-level analysis. With thought, you can no doubt name several people who fit each of these descriptions. And you can learn something about yourself in the process of trying to figure out which category best describes you. We would probably all like to think that we are maximizers, but, in truth, we are not. Still, with some ambition, some effort and some calculated risk-taking, we can all get closer to maximizing our performance, whatever potential and circumstances we have been given. It is ambition, effort and risk, aided by the practice of the various leadership traits I've considered here, that will keep us out of the ranks of the underachievers.

Exercises

You have been encouraged to view all of the films for the oft-stated purpose of observing the expressions and body language involved in particular leadership qualities being portrayed. Talking about what you've learned with your peers is also encouraged. In an effort to assist in the stimulating discussion that I hope will result, I offer the following exercises.

Interchange characters. In each of the films, replace the lead character or characters with the lead character from another film, and discuss how the new character would have behaved. For example, how would Erin behave as the lead character in *Apollo 13*? What might be the consequences of that behavior?

Rate achievement levels. Describe each of the leads as an underachiever, overachiever or maximizer. Discuss why you think the tag is justified.

Assess yourself. List, in order of strength, the leadership qualities you believe you possess. Ask your friends to assess you against the leadership capabilities you listed and perhaps even other qualities they come up with on their own. Compare the lists and discuss the differences. You may also consider whether or not your leadership strengths and weaknesses in the workplace differ from your leadership strengths and weaknesses in other roles that you play; if so, do the differences serve you well?

Make yourself a star. Put yourself in the lead roles in the scenes in the preceding chapters and describe how you would behave. Put one of your colleagues in the scene and predict how that person would react.

And the Award Goes To...

In the first chapter, I allowed as to how there are no secrets to leadership. It is hard work, and it is the learning and practice of the qualities explored in this book that will differentiate you in the competition. Leadership excellence is attainable, and I am gratified that you have chosen to spend some of your time using this book as one of your tools in your own personal pursuit of excellence.

As leaders and potential leaders, you are keenly aware that your most valuable commodity is your time. You can save it, waste it or spend it with various degrees of wisdom. I want you to know that I appreciate that fact also and thank you for spending some of your most valuable asset on this book. I hope that your investment of time provided you with a new lens through which you can observe leadership traits in the future. If so, then I have succeeded in my mission.

I started this book suggesting that "leadership" is difficult to define. After giving it much thought, I offer the following:

> *Leadership is inspiring others to exceed their*
> *perceived talents through guided empowerment.*

Without the ability to inspire, leaders cannot lead. And without guidance, empowerment invites anarchy.

This is my definition. I challenge each of you to create your own.

Ralph R. DiSibio

Printed in the United States
48088LVS00005B/139-1008

9 780977 927302